The Illustrated Lives of the Great Composers.

Debussy

DATE DUE

Omnibus Press
London/New York/Sydney

Cover design and art direction by Pearce Marchbank Studio.
Cover photography by Julian Hawkins.

© Paul Holmes 1989.
This edition published in 1989 by Omnibus Press, a division of Book Sales Limited.

Order No. OP45244
ISBN 0.7119.1752.3

Exclusive Distributors:
Book Sales Limited,
8/9 Frith Street,
London W1V 5TZ,
England.
Music Sales Pty Limited,
120 Rothschild Avenue,
Rosebery,
Sydney,
NSW 2018,
Australia.
Music Sales Corporation,
257 Park Avenue South,
New York,
N.Y. 10010
U.S.A.
To The Music Trade Only:
Music Sales Limited,
8/9 Frith Street,
London W1V 5TZ,
England.

Contents

1   Early Years   5

2   Study and Travel   10

3   Rome   23

4   The Bohemian   29

5   The Years of Pelléas   49

6   Success and Scandal   63

7   More Scandal   72

8   The Family Man   79

9   Travel and Seclusion   87

10 Return to the Theatre   95

11 In Black and White   109

12 Last Days   115

    Appendix   125

    Selected Bibliography   129

    Selective Listing of Works   130

    Index   133

1 Early Years

Manuel-Achille Debussy

Victorine Debussy

The modest china shop at 38 Rue au Pain in the small town of St Germain-en-Laye closed early on 22 August 1862. Although business was never very good, Manuel-Achille Debussy, the proprietor, had other problems to worry about. That day his wife Victorine had just given birth to their first child – a son whom they called Achille-Claude – and the baby's strange double forehead seemed to hint at a hydrocephalic deformity.

Whilst this petty bourgeois couple fretted, nearby Paris buzzed with activity. Along the fine new boulevards recently laid out by the order of their emperor, Napoleon III, carriages conveyed the fashionable to afternoon salons where virtuosi peformed Chopin, and Liszt's pot-pourris on operatic themes. Later the pleasure-seekers would hear the frothy operettas of Offenbach at the *Opéra-Comique*, or, if more seriously inclined, would visit the Paris *Opéra* where the grand operas of Meyerbeer, Halévy, Auber, and Gounod's newly acclaimed *Faust*, ruled the season. Wagner, whose *Tannhaüser* had failed so disastrously the previous year at the *Opéra*, would not cast his immense shadow over French music for some time, and music continued to veer between the frivolous and the severely classical for the remainder of the Second Empire.

Achille-Claude Debussy did not develop hydrocephalus and, despite his parents' fears, grew into a normal child, although his unusual forehead remained his most distinctive feature for the rest of his life. Two years after his birth a sister, Adèle, was born and, the china shop having failed, the Debussys moved to Clichy, on the outskirts of Paris, and then to the Rue Pigalle in Paris itself. Here Manuel flitted from one job to another whilst his wife continued to fuss over his son's health. An emotional woman, she sheltered him and never allowed him to attend school but, although not a cultured person, gave him all the elementary instruction he was to receive. In this protective environment, the child's love of the exquisite developed. His sister later wrote of his love of small objects, ornaments and, especially, butterflies which

Claude Debussy's
birthplace, 38 Rue au Pain,
St-Germain-en-Laye

he arranged in cases round the walls of his room. Her memoirs of him could not have been based on very close contact, however, for after her fifth year she and the three brothers Alfred, Emmanuel and Eugène, born after her, were entrusted to their maternal aunt, a certain Mme Rostan who preferred to affect the title Octavie de la Ferronnière. Only Achille-Claude remained for long in his parents' home.

Eugène died of meningitis as a baby, although the others survived. Mme Rostan was in an excellent position to help her poor relations due to the wealth of her lover, Achille-Antoine Arosa. When Achille-Claude was in his sixth year she took him from his suffocating Parisian home to spend the summer at the Arosa mansion near Cannes in the South of France. Achille-Claude later wrote of his visits:

I remember the railway that passed in front of the house and the sea that stretched as far as the horizon. Sometimes you could imagine that the railway came right out of the sea or went into it – whatever you prefer. There was also the Route d'Antibes with all its roses. I have never seen as many in one place in my life . . . There was also a Norwegian carpenter who sang – possibly Grieg – from morning to night . . .

Arosa was cultivated as well as rich and was especially fond of paintings which he collected enthusiastically. The young Debussy would have seen paintings by the Barbizon group, including Theodore Rousseau, Boudin and Corot in his collection. He also supported the struggling young artists later to be abused as 'Impressionists' and Debussy may even have seen some of them enjoying Arosa's hospitality. The light in the South of France is extraordinarily vivid and the colours consequently stronger than in Paris and this early exposure to colour and the techniques of Impressionism so influenced the young Debussy that he at first decided to become a painter. His father had determined that he should eventually join the Navy and to add to the confusion his aunt sent him for a few piano lessons with an Italian teacher in Cannes called Cerutti. The child was only seven, hardly an age when a future career could be definitely decided, and he continued to splash his paints and tinker at the piano in Paris and on holiday in Cannes for another two years. His father also made sure that he wore a small sailor's hat.

Although the Debussy home in Paris did not encourage an artistic vocation, Debussy *père* is said to have enjoyed light books, plays and operettas and, according to one account, he took his eldest son to London at this time where they heard Sullivan's *HMS Pinafore* performed. Despite his son referring to him in later years as 'an old waster' he seems to have been a pleasant, moderately easy-going man. Without permanent employment, he

Claude Debussy, a few months old, and (*right*) in 1867

Achille-Antoine Arosa

would spend time at the famous *Chat Noir* in Montmartre where his acquaintances included Charles de Sivry, the composer of operettas and cabaret songs, who worked as an accompanist there. No doubt in conversation he mentioned his son's interest in the piano and de Sivry decided to introduce the nine-year-old child to his mother, Mme Mauté de Fleurville, a pianist who had once studied with Chopin, had known Wagner, and whose salon attracted many prominent musicians of the age. She heard the boy play, 'But he must become a musician!' she declared and offered to give him lessons herself in preparation for the entrance examination to the Paris Conservatoire.

The years 1870 to 1873, when the young Debussy was studying with this famous lady, were ones of great trial to France and to

Mme de Fleurville personally. The Franco-Prussian war, which an opportunist Bismarck had launched on a scheming but unprepared Napoleon III in 1870, dragged on through 1871 and ended after a long siege of Paris in which many people starved. Napoleon III had been deposed, Paris evacuated by the government and most of its prominent citizens taken shelter in Versailles, leaving the ordinary people to set up barricades and declare the short-lived Commune. After the defeat and humiliation of France by Prussia, culminating in the declaration of the Prussian king Wilhelm as Kaiser of all Germany in Versailles' great Hall of Mirrors, France's new republic decided to end uncertainty by bloodily suppressing the Commune. Fighting lasted for two months in the streets of the capital and thousands died there or were subsequently shot.

The ten-year-old Debussy was in the thick of these upheavals, for his father took part in the Commune and was put in prison for a short while. The humiliation of France touched his son deeply and was to colour much of his attitude towards Germany in later years.

Mme Mauté de Fleurville

By the autumn of 1871 large areas of Paris were in ruins and Prussian soldiers were billeted everywhere. The frivolous Second Empire had ended but in her newly-reopened house Mme de Fleurville continued to coach the young Debussy, giving him instructions on pedal technique and reminiscing about Chopin. This lady, 'to whom I owe the little I know about the piano' as Debussy later modestly wrote, had much to put up with domestically at the time. Her daughter was married to the poet Paul Verlaine who had just introduced the seventeen-year-old poet Arthur Rimbaud to their home. Quite clearly there was a sexual relationship between the two, and as if this were not enough for Verlaine's long-suffering mother-in-law, Rimbaud's personal habits and opinions were designed to shock everyone, especially the bourgeoisie. It would be interesting to know what the ten-year-old Debussy made of Rimbaud the libertine and what influence this anarchic youth full of wild Symbolist poetry could have had on him. He later set Verlaine's poetry to music but not Rimbaud's, although deeply attracted by Symbolist ideas, and it must be assumed that he did not approve of an adolescent who scrawled *Merde à Dieu* on park benches, smoked hashish, disrupted a civilised home and drew Mme de Fleurville's son-in-law into a 'systematic derangement of the senses' in search of symbolic poetry.

The stormy Verlaine-Rimbaud relationship continued to distract Debussy's teacher until the young pianist's entry to the Conservatoire in October 1873. It is a tribute to her professionalism, as well as Debussy's talent, that she managed to

The Conservatoire, Paris

get him through the examination despite the divorce of her daughter and the eventual imprisonment of her ex-son-in-law earlier in the year for wounding Rimbaud with a revolver. Verlaine later praised her in his memoirs, calling her 'a charming soul, an instinctive and talented artist, an excellent musician of exquisite taste, intelligent and devoted to those she loved', so it is clear she could have borne little bitterness towards the man if he could pen such a glowing portrait of her as he declined still further into degradation.

But Debussy was about to rise. An awkward, yet prematurely wise child, he entered the Paris Conservatoire that autumn with high hopes of becoming a virtuoso pianist. Although looking like a bumpkin in his sailor's hat, he had a copy of Theodore de Banville's poems with him. Banville was Rimbaud's 'Dear Master', the editor of the influential literary journal *Parnasse Contemporain*, so the unusual literary influences of the previous three years had borne some lasting fruit for Debussy.

9

2 Study and Travel

Antoine Marmontel

Typically, the young man began his career by encountering conflict. His two professors could not have been more different. Albert Lavignac, his *solfège* teacher, was only 27 whereas Antoine Marmontel, who was in charge of the advanced piano class, was 57. Of the two, it was Lavignac who recognised the young Debussy's extraordinary gifts, most notably in the specialised ear-training of his own discipline. He spent long hours with the boy after class, discussing his strange questions which seemed to undermine the whole theory of music, and playing through revolutionary music with him, including Wagner's *Tannhäuser*, still not accepted by French critical minds or audiences alike.

This friendship helped Debussy endure the more severe Marmontel whose emphasis on classical technical exercises and whose almost wholly didactic mind caused a great deal of friction between them. Debussy loved to experiment openly with bizarre chords and unresolved tonalities; 'he used to amaze us with his weird playing' fellow-student Gabriel Pierné later wrote. He also spent much time playing Chopin, Mozart and the eccentric Alkan for whose music he retained a lifelong affection, rather than the scales and theoretical studies dictated by his tutor. 'He is not fond of the piano, but he is fond of music' was Marmontel's summing up of Debussy, showing how incapable he was of understanding a boy who was later to write some of the finest piano music of all time.

Marmontel was, however, right in his very limited view. Debussy did not have the temperament of that kind of person his tutor was paid to produce: the virtuoso. Many years later Debussy wrote a review in which he said all there is to be said of such empty display for its own sake:

The attraction of the virtuoso for the public is very like the circus for the crowd. There is always the hope that something dangerous might happen: M. Ysaÿe may play the violin with M. Colonne on his shoulders, or M. Pugno may conclude his piece by lifting the piano with his teeth.

To add to this rebellious attitude, he was 'reserved', 'sullen' and 'generally late' as an older student, Camille Bellaigue, wrote in a telling account:

'Here you are at last!' Marmontel would say as a small, sickly-looking lad came in . . . He wore a belted tunic and carried in his hand a kind of cap . . . like a sailor's cap. Nothing about him suggested the artist, present or future; neither his face, nor his speech, nor his playing . . . He was one of the youngest of the pianists, but by no means one of the best. I remember, in particular, the nervous habit he had of emphasising the strong beats by a kind of panting or raucous breathing . . . He was not popular with his fellow students.

Emile Durand

Debussy's sensibilities enabled him eventually to win first prize in Lavignac's class, but he struggled to attain distinction in Marmontel's. At the age of twelve he played Chopin's Second Piano Concerto in a Conservatoire competition, 'To youth, much must be forgiven,' the critic of the influential newspaper *Le Temps* patronised, although he received a second honourable mention at the time. In 1875 he did better with Chopin's *Ballade No. 2*, but Beethoven defeated him the following year and it was not until 1877, at the age of 14, that he received second prize playing the first movement of a Schumann sonata. The following years showed no improvement and, despite the threats of his father who made him practise long hours, it became apparent that his son would never be the money-spinning virtuoso he had hoped for, although by then he had found permanent employment of his own with a firm of accountants where he was to remain for the rest of his life, so relieving the family of some of its financial strain.

As the pressure was taken off Debussy's studies with Marmontel he concentrated on his first attempts at composition by setting some poems of Theodore de Banville's and improvising strange preludes. He also entered Emile Durand's harmony class in 1876. Nothing could have been less auspicious for the future composer. According to another pupil, one of Debussy's few friends, Maurice Emmanuel, Durand 'liked neither music, teaching, nor his pupils . . . If, when the class was over, one of the pupils would play over to his friends some composition he had attempted, Durand would slam the lid of the piano on his fingers and say: "You'd do better to work at your progressions!"'

But even the pedantic and mediocre hack Durand was secretly fascinated by Debussy's arrogant disdain for the rules. Another pupil, Antoine Barrès wrote that:

At the end of the lesson, when he had examined all our exercises with scrupulous care he would linger over the correction of young Claude's work with almost epicurean enjoyment. Severe criticisms and angry

Claude Debussy in 1875

pencil marks rained upon the pupil's head and music paper. However . . . he re-read in silent concentration the pages he had so cruelly mutilated, murmuring with an enigmatic smile: 'Of course, it is all utterly unorthodox, but still, it is very ingenious.'

Maurice Emmanuel preserved many of Debussy's more unusual improvisations in a notebook, so fascinated was he by their audacity.

The years of study from 1873 to 1879 were marked by few outside influences on the adolescent Debussy. Although with his early love and knowledge of art and the unorthodox, he must have been aware of the first Impressionist exhibitions held in a private studio in 1874 and 1875 and mocked by the Parisians of the Third Republic almost universally, one critic suggesting that these luminous canvases with their disregard for detail drove people to bite passers-by in the street! Debussy's only other stimuli, according to his friend and fellow-pupil Paul Vidal, were the light operas performed at the *Opéra-Comique* – Offenbach, Delibes and the now little-known Pessard were his favourites. On the more

12

serious side, he held Berlioz in great esteem, was interested in the Belgian composer César Franck who held such sway at the Conservatoire, the prolific Saint-Saëns, and showed such enthusiasm for Lalo's ballet *Namouna* that he was ejected from the theatre. He also admired the lush operas of Massenet, then so much in vogue, especially *Manon* and *Hérodiade*. Although he later outgrew these influences, he maintained an ambiguous respect for Massenet's treatment of the French language with its mellifluous recitative, later writing: 'his influence on contemporary music is obvious,' although also stating that he seemed to be: 'the victim of the fluttering fans of his admirers . . . he yearned to reserve for himself the beating of those perfumed wings, unfortunately, he might as well have tried to tame a cloud of butterflies.' In these few words Debussy caught the vapid enthusiasms of Paris after the Franco-Prussian War, a place of unstable governments and frivolous entertainments.

One thread ran through all Debussy's youthful interests – the

Le Printemps by Pissarro, commissioned by Achille Arosa

desire to be wholly French – for, although he admired Mozart, Schumann and the Francophile Chopin, his taste for composers of other nationalities, even Beethoven, was hampered by what he regarded as the 'tedious working-out' demanded by classical forms, and he held Beethoven largely responsible for the 'laborious and stilted compositions which we are accustomed to call symphonies', especially the French symphony of the time.

Debussy continued to study unhappily in Durand's class until 1880, producing unorthodox harmonic exercises, fugues and canons, and continued perfecting an individual piano technique under Marmontel's direction. Then a chance came his way to escape briefly from academic discipline and broaden his horizons. In the summer of 1880, largely through the recommendation of Marmontel, Debussy met Nadezhda von Meck.

This extraordinary Russian lady is best remembered for her association with the composer Tchaikovsky whose patroness she remained for over sixteen years on the sole condition that they should never meet, despite exchanging the most intimate letters.

13

After the death of her mining engineer husband, she had inherited a large fortune which she spent on her great love, music, touring Europe with her eleven children and her private trio of musicians. Debussy was now contracted to join her as pianist during the summer months. He arrived at the Château de Chenonceaux at Interlaken, Switzerland on 8 July 1880 and Mme von Meck wrote enthusiastically to Tchaikovsky:

Two days ago a young pianist arrived from Paris where he has just graduated from the Conservatoire with the first prize in Marmontel's class. I engaged him for the summer to give lessons to the children, accompanying Julia's singing and play four hands with myself. This young man plays well, his technique is brilliant but he lacks any personal expression. He is yet too young, says he is twenty, but looks sixteen.

Debussy seems to have covered his awkwardness and inexperience with a series of white lies; not only was he only eighteen, but he had not won first prize in piano at all, simply in

Mme von Meck's personal trio: Debussy, Danilchenko and Pachulsky

Florence

score-reading, and he had not graduated, but had several more years of study before him. Later, Mme von Meck called him 'a typical product of the Paris boulevard' but his affected love of Tchaikovsky's music was more than compensation for any gaucheness in his manner, 'He is delighted with your music,' she wrote to Tchaikovsky from the South of France where they next stayed, and Debussy is known to have arranged some dances from *Swan Lake* which were published soon after. Later they travelled to Rome and, in September, to Florence where Mme von Meck sent one of Debussy's compositions to Tchaikovsky for appraisal. Tchaikovsky thought this early *Danse bohémienne* for piano 'a very nice thing, but altogether too short' and declared that the whole form was 'bungled'. Tactless though this may have been, it did not prevent Debussy from writing a full scale *Piano Trio in G* at Florence and several songs, all, according to Mme von Meck, 'reminiscent of Massenet'.

The young Frenchman does not seem to have impressed the von Meck children very greatly although the times they spent together were pleasant and relaxed. Nicholas von Meck, one of the eldest, later wrote of him:

The little Frenchman arrived, dark, thin, sarcastic, and gave everyone amusing nicknames. For instance, he called our plump teacher 'little hippopotamus on holiday' and we in turn nicknamed him 'impetuous Achille' . . . Once we walked past the Villa Medici [in Rome] where the best students of the Conservatoire . . . reside for a year at the expense of the French government. One of us, pointing to the villa, said to Debussy: 'This is your future home.' It was interesting to see how longingly he looked back at the Villa Medici. From Rome we went to Florence . . .

Ernest Guiraud

César Franck

and from there in October, Debussy returned to his studies in Paris. On leaving us he was very sad and my mother had to comfort him . . .

After spending time with the cosmopolitan von Mecks and visiting Florence and Rome, Debussy's return to the Conservatoire must have been a depressing experience, especially since he found that he could not gain much from César Franck, in whose composition and organ class he now enrolled. However, a

Mme Vasnier

change to Ernest Guiraud's composition class soon afterwards proved to be exactly what he needed. Guiraud appreciated the novel ideas of his pupil and the two soon became good friends, enjoying expeditions into the night-life of Montmartre together, where they drank, played billiards and smoked endlessly during long artistic conversations in the cafés. Guiraud was a mainstream French composer in the tradition of Bizet and Massenet. He had written recitatives for *Carmen* as well as finishing Offenbach's only successful grand opera *The Tales of Hoffmann*, and it was through his tolerant supervision that Debussy began to sense his own unique gifts as a composer. A small income also came his way when Paul Vidal gained him the post of accompanist to the choral society *La Concordia*, whose president, Charles Gounod, the composer of the famous *Faust*, took a liking to him. Through his influence, other work came his way and it was whilst working as an accompanist for the singing teacher Mme Moreau-Sainti that he met one of her pupils, the wife of an architect: Mme Vasnier. She and Debussy felt a close affinity from the beginning and during the next few years Debussy was to be a frequent guest at the Vasnier home in Paris and at their country retreat in Ville d'Avray nearby. Mme Vasnier's daughter later wrote a description of Debussy as he appeared at their flat in the Rue de Constantinople:

He was a big, beardless boy with strongly marked features and thick, black, curly hair which he wore flat on his forehead, but in the evening, when his hair had become untidy – which suited him much better – my parents used to say that he looked like some Medieval Florentine type. His face was interesting. His eyes were especially striking. His personality made itself felt. His hands were strong and bony and his fingers square . . . As he had little support [from his family] he asked my parents if he could come and work at our house, and thenceforth he was admitted as one of the family. I can still see him in the little drawing room on the fifth floor . . . where for five years he wrote most of his compositions. He used to come there nearly every evening, often in the afternoons too, leaving behind him the unfinished pages which were placed on a little table as soon as he arrived. He used to compose at the piano . . . or at times walking about the room. He would improvise for a long time, then walk up and down humming, with the everlasting cigarette in his mouth, or else rolling tobacco and paper in his fingers. When he had found what he wanted, he began to write. He made few corrections, but he spent a long time working things out in his head and at the piano before he wrote. He was rarely satisfied with his work . . . He was very quick to take offence and extremely sensitive. The slightest thing put him in good humour or made him sullen or angry. He was very unsociable and never hid his displeasure when my parents invited friends, for he did not often allow himself to be with strangers . . . he was original though rather unpolished, but very charming with people he liked.

Although moody, she wrote, he could entertain them all with

The von Meck family,
c 1878

parodies and comic songs. He was a bad loser at cards but a skilful croquet player at their Ville d'Avray home where he and her mother would go through the songs he had written there.

Debussy spent far more time at the Vasniers' than in the rather limited cultural atmosphere of his parents' home where he only returned to sleep in the evenings. M. Vasnier must have been a very tolerant husband for it is clear now that the relationship that existed between the moody eighteen-year-old and his young wife was emotional and possibly sexual. Despite this, he treated the young Debussy with extreme friendliness, introducing him to his library and recommending books which the largely uneducated Debussy read voraciously. He is known to have spent much time with a dictionary, filling in the yawning gaps in his knowledge. It was at the Vasniers' that he first encountered the poetry of Stéphane Mallarmé, the leading Symbolist poet of the age, and he was fascinated by its attempts to include musical ideas in the verse. He was also reacquainted with Verlaine in the more decorous world of his poems, and set a number of them to music including an early version of the song cycle *Fêtes galantes*. He dedicated these to Mme Vasnier in the most playfully sentimental manner: 'These songs, which she alone has made live, and which will lose their enchanting grace if they are never again to come from her singing fairy lips.'

18

Having entered Guiraud's composition class, it is clear that Debussy's heart was now set on being a composer foremost and, despite his adolescent nonconformity, he took the conventional step of preparing for the *Prix de Rome* competition. Victory in this would ensure that he could stay at the Villa Medici for three years, that same villa at which he had gazed so longingly in the von Mecks' company the year before. In order to be considered he had to write a cantata on the usual formal text, but consideration of this was shelved in the summer of 1881 when he joined the von Meck entourage as pianist once more.

'My little Frenchman is anxious to come here,' Mme von Meck wrote to Tchaikovsky from the Ukraine and so Debussy travelled to Russia to meet her in July. He stayed at their home near Podolsk until September when the restless von Mecks travelled to Moscow.

Although its polite society conversed in French and aped Paris fashions, this ancient city must have seemed rough and ready to the young 'product of the Paris boulevards'. Being devoted to the cult of Tchaikovsky, Mme von Meck had little time for the Russian nationalist composers – Rimsky-Korsakov, Mussorgsky, Balakirev, Borodin and Cui – who had banded themselves together as 'The Five', so Debussy's contact with their seminal music was limited. Besides, Mussorgsky had died of alcoholism

Moscow

only a few months earlier. The only other composer she admired was Anton Rubinstein. The brilliant literary and political ideas of the time probably made no impact on the von Meck salon either, and it was left to Mme von Meck's eldest son, the dissolute Vladimir, to show Debussy something of Bohemian Moscow by taking him on drinking expeditions round the cabarets – an occupation dear to Vladimir's heart. It is known that Debussy played much of Tchaikovsky's music with his employer and that he obtained some copies of Borodin's songs and one of Rimsky-Korsakov's early operas, but his time was too limited to delve much deeper.

Richard Wagner in 1880

After his return to Paris, Debussy became increasingly unruly at the Conservatoire, worldly influences having inflamed his intolerant, faintly aristocratic outlook. He ceased to call himself Achille-Claude, becoming just Claude, but compensated this for a short time by signing himself de Bussy and assuming condescending airs towards both fellow-students and teachers alike. It was probably due to Guiraud's friendship and belief in his abilities that he was not expelled, as were some of his contemporaries for far less outspoken rebellions against academic conventions. At this time, although straining at the leash, he accepted Guiraud's advice and produced only academic compositions as preliminary to the *Prix de Rome* competition. Such works as *Salut, Printemps* and an *Intermezzo* based on a poem by Heine exist as testimony to an original mind fettered by conventions it longed to overthrow. These years saw the young composer growing in musical stature, still frequenting the Vasniers' liberal household where he wrote various forgotten works including a *Nocturne* and *Scherzo* for violin and piano – which Mme Vasnier arranged to be publicly performed in 1882 – and returning once more to join the von Meck tours. In 1882 he is believed to have visited Moscow once again and thence on to Vienna and Venice. It is thought that Debussy heard a performance of *Tristan und Isolde* in Vienna and the impression this startling music must have made on him at the time cannot be underestimated as it was entirely unknown at the Conservatoire. Some accounts also say that Debussy met Wagner in Venice, although it must have been only a formal visit as the old master of Bayreuth was at that time in bad health and was to die shortly afterwards.

On returning to Paris, Debussy began work on the composition of a cantata for the 1883 *Prix de Rome* competition, and continued to disrupt the Conservatoire. On one occasion he is reported to have attempted to reproduce the sounds of buses on the piano at one of Guiraud's classes: 'What are you so shocked about?' he shouted at his embarrassed fellow-students, 'Can't you listen to chords without knowing their status and destination? Where do they come from? Whither are they going? What does it matter? Listen: that's enough. If you can't make head or tail of it, go and tell *Monsieur le Directeur* that I am ruining your ears.' Such arrogance was the natural result of Debussy's attempts to coin a new musical language close to his deepest feelings; as a fellow-student, Raymond Bonheur, later said of him: 'He would rather have agreed to make counterfeit money than to write three bars of music without feeling an irresistible craving to do so . . . He was extremely sensitive to the opinion of a few . . . but supremely indifferent to the favours of the crowd . . .'

His attempt at the *Prix de Rome* of 1883 – the cantata *Le Gladiateur* – won second prize, despite being a work totally unworthy of the rebellious composer's aspirations. Paul Vidal, the composer's friend, narrowly beat him, but there was no animosity between the two, a celebration even being held at Debussy's home which Paul Vidal much later reported in an article:

At the end of 1883 I carried off the first prize . . . while Debussy obtained the second . . . this event was celebrated in the Debussy family by a meal of which I have the happiest memories. I was treated like a child of the house. Ernest Guiraud presided over this little family fête . . . Mme Debussy was a mother passionately devoted to her son, very 'exalted'; each letter that she received from her son during his journey [to Russia] was a real event in her life. She was very kind and spoiled me a great deal; she was also an excellent cook, and liked to make delicious desserts which also flattered the well-developed gastronomical tastes of Debussy . . . This couple belonged to a very modest class but . . . were interested in everything and were abreast of the times . . .

Debussy's disappointment was obvious to his friends, but he had so narrowly missed the first prize that he was persuaded to try once more the following year. He began work on a comedy by Banville entitled *Diane aux Bois*, but Guiraud suggested that he put it aside as it was not *Prix de Rome* material. During this period, the twenty-year-old composer became so contemptuous of the Conservatoire and his timid fellow-students that he was eventually called before the Registrar to explain himself, 'What rule do you follow?' the irate official demanded. 'My pleasure,' Debussy replied superciliously, sending his superior white and speechless with rage.

It was only due, once more, to the intercession of Guiraud that Debussy was not immediately expelled, and it was Guiraud who now guided his technique to such a pitch of self-assurance that he was able to compose *L'Enfant prodigue*, a cantata based on the story of the Prodigal Son. It owed much to the influence of Massenet, but with it he finally won the *Prix de Rome* in 1884.

Debussy later recalled this moment of triumph:

My happiest impressions connected with the *Prix de Rome* were independent of it. I was on the Pont des Arts awaiting the result of the competition and watching with delight the scurrying of the little Seine steamers. I was quite calm, having forgotten all emotion due to anything Roman, so seductive was the charm of the gay sunshine playing on the ripples, a charm which keeps those delightful idlers, who are the envy of Europe, hour after hour on the bridges. Suddenly someone tapped me on the shoulder and said breathlessly: 'You've won the prize!' Believe me or believe me not, I can assure you that all my pleasure vanished! I saw in a flash the boredom, the vexations inevitably incident to the slightest official recognition. Besides, I felt that I was no longer free. These impressions soon faded: we cannot be insensible of that little ray of provisional glory which the *Prix de Rome* gives: and when I reached the Villa Medici in 1885, I almost thought I must be that darling of the gods told of in ancient legends.

Gounod had embraced Debussy after hearing *L'Enfant prodigue* saying 'My child, you have genius,' and the critic of *Le Figaro* wrote that Debussy was: 'a musician who is destined to meet with a great deal of praise . . . and plenty of abuse . . . The very first bars of his score reveal a courageous nature and an outstanding personality.'

Tearful farewells were made with his family and the Vasniers (especially Mme Vasnier) and Debussy set off in January 1885 with all his youthful trepidation to spend three years in Rome.

3 Rome

The ancient city of Rome had only been the capital of a united kingdom of Italy for fifteen years when Debussy arrived there to live. For centuries previously it had been dominated by the Pope as temporal ruler, and the heavy weight of his moral authority hung heavily over the city although he had been forced to isolate himself in the Vatican. After Paris, it would have seemed stifling, provincial and faintly old-fashioned.

Although the Villa Medici itself, at which Debussy had gazed so longingly in the company of the von Mecks, was a Renaissance gem dating from 1557 and set in magnificent gardens, Debussy found no comfort there. Being winter, it rained almost continuously at first. Debussy wrote to the Vasniers:

Here I am in this abominable villa . . . My friends came to meet me at Monte Rotondo where the six of us slept in one dirty little room. If you only knew how changed they are! None of their good-hearted friendly ways of Paris. They're stiff and impressed with their own importance – too much *Prix de Rome* about them.

In the evening when I arrived at the villa, I played my cantata which was well-received by some, but not by the musicians.

I don't mind. The artistic atmosphere and camaraderie that we are told about seem to be very exaggerated. With one or two exceptions, it is difficult to talk to people here, and when I hear their ordinary conversation I cannot help thinking of the talks we used to have that opened my mind to so many things. Then the people here are so very egotistic . . . I've tried hard to work but I can't.

Writing again to the Vasniers he said: 'I dislocate my brain with no results except to make myself feverish.'

Debussy had to sleep in a large gloomy room which he shared with six other students and which they nicknamed 'The Etruscan Tomb'. The company he complained of, which included his old friends Paul Vidal and Gabriel Pierné from Conservatoire days, continuously bickered with each other about pretentious artistic

The Villa Medici, Rome

Claude Debussy with his companions at the Villa Medici, 1885

theories and the food was so bad that Debussy later complained that he 'narrowly escaped poisoning'. In his later account of this period Debussy wrote:

The conversations at the table very much resemble the gossip at a *table d'hôte*, and it would be idle to imagine that new theories of art, or even the burning dreams of the old masters are discussed . . . Intercourse with Roman society is virtually non-existent, since its inaccessibility equals its self-sufficiency, and the youthful and thoroughly French independence of a student's mind consorts ill with Roman frigidity.

Isolated in this 'compulsory barracks', as he also called it, in which he had little sympathy for either students or the director Cabat, who was an artist, Debussy struggled to write his first *envoi* – the work every student had to send each year to Paris to confirm his progress. The text chosen, *Zuleima*, based on a translation of

24

verses by Heine, soon defeated him. They were 'great only in their length' he opined, 'my music would be submerged by their weight.' He next attempted to recast Banville's *Diane aux Bois* as an opera but soon discovered that he had 'undertaken a work beyond my powers. As there are no precedents . . . I must create new forms.' In a state of artistic crisis, dissatisfied with everything he attempted, and longing to write the music that he could only glimpse within him, he sent the unfinished *Zuleima* to the committee of the *Académie* who presided over the *Prix de Rome*. Predictably, they found it 'incomprehensible' and 'bizarre'.

Although he found consolation in reading Verlaine, Baudelaire, Shakespeare and the newly fashionable Pre-Raphaelite Rossetti aloud with his companions, and was photographed and painted in a suitably aloof pose, the inner insecurity of the man showed itself in a letter which only came to light twenty years after his death. In it, he confessed that Mme Vasnier had a lasting hold on his emotions and his inspiration:

I must tell you that there has been no change in me during the last two months, if anything, my feelings have only been intensified during that time. I am bound to acknowledge their force, because in the absence of what inspires them I am unable to live – for when one's imagination will no longer allow itself to be controlled, one might just as well not be alive. As I have told you before, I have been too accustomed only to want things and conceive them *through her* . . . I know this is not following the advice you gave me to try to reduce this passion, which I know is mad, to a lasting friendship, but it's because it is so mad that it prevents me from being reasonable. Thinking seriously about it not only makes it worse, but almost convinces me that I have not sacrificed enough to this love.

At last, with an 'indescribable feeling of being out of my proper atmosphere', longing for an artistic originality that he could not grasp, 'too enamoured of my freedom, too fond of my own ideas' as he wrote to the Vasniers, he accepted an invitation to spend the summer at the seaside villa of a Count Josef Primoli at Fiumicino, but he felt just as much out of his depth there and soon returned to Rome with a feeling of frustration.

Yet, despite these traumas, he was making other useful contacts. Although not interested in Italian opera, he met Leoncavallo, then making a difficult living by teaching, but soon to write the world-famous *verismo* opera *I Pagliacci*, and through him he was introduced to Boito, the librettist, and composer of *Mefistofele*. He in turn introduced Debussy to Verdi, the most important Italian composer of his day. According to Debussy, he met the seventy-year-old composer at his villa in Sant' Agathe where he was working in his garden like the peasant he pretended to be. Conversation over lunch was polite, but Debussy was not to

Franz Liszt

be influenced by these men. He was more impressed by Liszt whom he met at the home of Liszt's pupil, Sgambati. Formerly the greatest piano virtuoso of the age, but then also in his seventies and in semi-religious orders, the Abbé Liszt still 'seemed to make the pedal breathe', as Debussy later said. The 'breathing' pedal was later to become a hallmark of Debussy's own piano works. The old maestro played Saint-Saëns' *Variations on a Theme of Beethoven* with Sgambati and, on a later visit with Paul Vidal, Debussy played Chabrier's *Valses Romantiques* for Liszt; but the friendship was not to develop, for Liszt died the following year.

Liszt in piano technique and Wagner in composition – the twin spirits of the nineteenth century's 'New Music' opposing Classicism – were to dominate Debussy for a while. He played through the whole of *Tristan und Isolde* at the Villa Medici several times and became, by his own admission, 'a Wagnerian to the pitch of forgetting the simple rules of courtesy'. As such, he was only echoing a movement that was dominating European music at the time, but it brought him into head-on collision with Cabat's successor as director, Hébert, another painter who hated Wagner and idolised Mozart.

Debussy found solace in the art galleries and museums of Rome and in the Commedia dell' Arte of the Roman streets with its stock

Detail from Botticelli's *Primavera*

but ambiguous cast of Harlequin, Columbine and Pulchinello. He also wandered into the little church of San Maria dell' Anima where he heard masses by Palestrina and Lassus whose use of counterpoint seemed magical to him after studying only dry academic exercises in the form. As he wrote to the Vasniers: 'These were the only occasions when my musical feelings were at all awakened,' and, in comparison with the severe beauty of this music, 'that of Gounod and Co seems the product of hysterical mysticism, and sounds like a sinister farce.'

After repeatedly writing to the Vasniers that he could no longer bear Rome, Debussy finally flung himself at the feet of Hébert (literally) and, weeping theatrically, threatened to kill himself if he was not allowed to leave immediately for Paris. Faced with such a performance, the director, who had a genuine liking for his dramatic charge, could hardly refuse, so Debussy arrived in Paris at the beginning of 1886. Once there, he was able to indulge his paradoxical liking for 'Manet and Offenbach' as he wrote in one letter, take up with the Vasniers again and visit all of his old café haunts where he met the music publisher Emile Baron who in turn introduced him to the editor of *La Revue Indépendante*, the influential Symbolist magazine. This escape was only to last a few weeks however. Perhaps growing weary of the young man's infatuation for his wife, M. Vasnier soon persuaded Debussy, who had no real means of support, to return to Rome.

Back at the Villa Medici, he felt once more 'the majestic *ennui* which is part of the air one breathes' and continued his aimless round of sightseeing, returning at night to sleep amongst his 'gaolers' for the rest of the year. In this mood he started work on two more *envois*: *La Damoiselle élue*, based on a translation of Rossetti's static Pre-Raphaelite poem, *The Blessed Damozel*, and *Printemps*, inspired by Botticelli's painting *Primavera*. It is possible that he also wrote part of a *Fantaisie* for piano and orchestra. *Printemps* was the only work finished in time for despatch for Paris and he seemed to have a genuine enthusiasm for it. He wrote to Emile Baron:

I should like to express the slow and miserable birth of beings and things in nature, their gradual blossoming and finally the joy of being born into some new life. All this is without a programme for I despise all music that has to follow some literary text that one happens to have got hold of. So you will understand how very suggestive the music will have to be – I am doubtful if I shall be able to do it as I wish.

Despite rebelling against literary texts – a feeling quite natural after his failure with Banville and Heine and possibly reflecting problems with the Rossetti poem – his new inspiration from art produced a successful tone poem in two parts with wordless choir.

Claude Debussy in Rome, 1885

Although it showed the influence of Wagner and Franck, it also revealed unmistakably original signs of the mature composer, but through a series of unexplained accidents, the score was burned at the bookbinders and the *Académie* in Paris had to judge its merits on a thinly rescored version. 'M. Debussy does not transgress through dullness or triteness,' the *Académie* worthies reported on seeing the work, 'on the contrary, he shows a rather over-pronounced taste for the unusual . . . He should beware of this vague Impressionism which is one of the most dangerous enemies of artistic truth . . . The *Académie* awaits and expects something better from such a gifted musician as M. Debussy.'

The term 'Impressionism' could hardly have been a more damning one from the academic viewpoint, the Impressionist painters of the period receiving nothing but scorn from academics and public alike for their seeming abandonment of form, but by 1887 Debussy had outgrown the strictures of his teachers and cared nothing for the public whom he regarded with an aristocratic disdain acquired through long exposure to the finer things of life. Shortly after receiving this report on his work, he wrote to M. Vasnier:

I'd rather do twice as much work in Paris than drag out this life here. I am leaving on Saturday and shall arrive in Paris on Monday morning. Don't, I beg of you, be too hard with me. Your friendship will be all I have.

So after only two, instead of the usual three, years at the Villa Medici, Debussy left for Paris in the spring of 1887 to face an uncertain future as a freelance musician.

4 The Bohemian

Debussy arrived in Paris with little more than his manuscripts and a few Japanese *objets d'art*. He had no visible means of support and had to rely on the help of friends to establish himself at first. At twenty-five he did not feel able to return to his family home so drifted from friends to one set of lodgings after another. The Vasniers helped him with money, contacts and advice, but even these old friends, so close before, were no longer really intimate. 'He had evolved and so had we,' their daughter wrote, 'reticent and unsociable, he no longer felt at home . . . Then little by little, having made new acquaintances himself he no longer came and we never saw him again.'

These new acquaintances included the foremost literary and artistic figures of the time but, typically, not many musicians, although he was still officially under the aegis of the Conservatoire and met his old teacher Guiraud often. Through these connections freelance teaching and arrangement work came his way although he does not seem to have performed in public. He composed steadily, however. In addition to *La Damoiselle élue*, he wrote short salon pieces for piano as well as songs inspired by his new literary interests.

At this time the main focus of the Parisian literary world was, ironically for Debussy, 87, Rue de Rome. There, every Tuesday, in the flat of the Symbolist poet and teacher Stéphane Mallarmé, who had only just published his influential *Poésies*, young writers, artists and musicians would rub shoulders with such men as the witty and irascible artist James McNeil Whistler, of whom Ruskin had said that he had 'flung a paintpot in the public's face' with his daring and original brand of Impressionism. Manet was also there, and Odilon Redon; Verlaine and other poets including Jules Laforge, Paul Valéry, Paul Claudel with André Gide and the fantastic Villiers de Lisle Adam. But Mallarmé was the acknowledged leader of the group. According to one disciple he had:

Boulevard Montmartre: effet de nuit by Pissarro, 1897

a pleasant voice . . . and speech as subtle as it was inexhaustible, raising every subject to the heights . . . literature, music, art, life and even items from the daily press, finding hidden similarities between things . . . The universe was made simple when he drew it together in the world of dreams, as the sea is concentrated in the murmur of a seashell.

Amongst the ideas he taught was one that Debussy found especially stimulating – that the Symbolist artist should empty his innermost being so that he could become a vessel for outside stimuli and sensations. He was to be like a fantastically decorated mirror in a room. The Symbolist enshrined pure receptivity.

It is probably true that nearly anyone who was or aspired to be anyone in the artistic world of Paris passed at one time or another through this famous flat. There, the other great idea that struck Debussy was that of a synthesis of the arts. Music, painting and literature could be thought of in each other's terms; the vowels, according to Rimbaud's sonnet, had colours; Huysmans, in his influential novel depicting the supremacy of the artificial *À Rebours*, described a 'Symphony of odours'; to Mallarmé, words had musical qualities and poems could be composed like a piece of

Stéphane Mallarmé by
Manet

music; and Whistler gave musical titles to his paintings:
symphonies in grey or white, nocturnes in red and gold. Yet the
music these artists aspired to was not the music of France – the
established figures of Gounod, Franck, Saint-Saëns and their
contemporaries, or the younger musicians Chausson, d'Indy,
Dukas, Fauré or the barely-known Debussy, but Wagner whose
belated conquest of Paris was now almost complete.

Wagner's shadow lay everywhere. He had broken music down
into indefinite harmonies which seemed to reach out to the world
of longings so important to Mallarmé and his Symbolist followers.
He had attempted a synthesis of the arts at his specially
constructed theatre at Bayreuth and many of his music dramas
inhabited the shadowy Medieval world of myth and legend that
Pre-Raphaelism admired. Literary obeisance before him was total
and at the famous *Lamoureux*, *Pasdeloup* and *Colonne* concerts
musical Paris fell down at his feet and worshipped as well. Mock-
Wagnerian operas were written by Frenchmen as different as
Chausson (*Le Roi Arthus*) and Chabrier (*Gwendoline*) so Debussy,
who had long admired Wagner, began his *Five Baudelaire Songs* in

31

La Revue wagnérienne,
May 1885. Lithography by
Fantin-Latour

Opposite page:
Gabrielle Dupont (Gaby):
photograph by Pierre Louÿs

Edgar Allan Poe

1887 with more than a trace of Wagner in the style.

In addition to these influences, that of Japanese art with its economy of line, and the poems and tales of Edgar Allan Poe with their heightened sense of extraordinary states of mind, added to the cultural stew. Mallarmé was just then completing his translations of the influential American author and called him in his poem, *Hommage à E. A. Poe*: 'the poet who lifts up his century with a naked sword', whilst Odilon Redon was producing his curious dream-pictures inspired by Poe's world. Debussy was so infatuated with Poe that, as André Suarès wrote to Romain Rolland in 1890: 'M. Claude Debussy . . . is working on a symphony that will unfold psychological ideas based on the stories of Poe, in particular, *The Fall of the House of Usher*.' Nothing came of this symphony but this is the first mention of an obsession that was to dog Debussy for the rest of his life.

At first, Debussy was only a shy, rather awkward spectator, especially at Mallarmé's flat, but his mind was a maelstrom of possibilities as he sampled each new idea and influence in turn. And he did not stay still. According to one account he set off in 1887 to Vienna, which Brahms had once called 'the musician's holy city'. There, he is thought to have met Brahms who, although refusing to see him at first, later softened and showed him some kindness, even taking him to see a performance of *Carmen*, although quite what such diverse personalities as the fifty-four-year-old Brahms and the gauche twenty-five-year-old Debussy had in common is hard to imagine, especially since Brahms was hardly well-disposed towards the French.

Debussy also visited London that year. This, the largest city in the world, seemed to fascinate the French who gazed with envy at its industrial might and its power radiating outward to an enormous empire that they had tried to emulate by annexing new territories in Africa and South-East Asia. Some, like Zola, were to find refuge from the political upheavals of France in a tolerant although ossified political system, or inspiration, like Rimbaud and Verlaine who were fascinated by London's appalling slums and rigid puritanism. Others, like Debussy, were drawn to the Aesthetic movement led by Oscar Wilde, or to the Pre-Raphaelites which Debussy greatly admired, emulating their voguish decadence by adopting flowing ties and outrageous hats. His recently completed tribute to this movement – the delicate oratorio *La Damoiselle élue* – seemed the ideal work to interest London publishers Novello's. But although many Frenchmen were pronounced Anglophiles, the fashion for things English having hit Paris as early as the 1870s, London did not have the same interest in France, least of all French music. Gilbert and Sullivan operettas, which Bernard Shaw remarked sounded oddly

Pierre Louÿs

churchy after Offenbach, were the most frivolous form of music London enjoyed outside the music halls. Brahms was considered modern and his English disciples Stanford, Parry and early Elgar vied with ponderously re-orchestrated Handel and Mendelssohn's oratorios for the attention of serious concert-goers, the French being considered 'too light'. As late as 1907, Debussy was to write: 'I would say that the English only have an interest in official music which has so far been provided by Handel and Sullivan.'

Debussy did meet Parry, then Director of the Royal College of Music, but this was to be no meeting of minds and he was unable to place his work with Novello's or any other publisher. Apart from seeing the paintings of Turner, which Debussy admired for their early Impressionism, the trip was a failure and the young composer soon returned to Paris.

It was in Paris that Debussy spent most of his time between 1887 and 1889, and it was there that he met his first openly-acknowledged lover, Gabrielle Dupont, the famous 'green-eyed Gaby'. She was a vivacious blonde who fitted in well with Debussy's circle of artistic acquaintances and the two set up home together, first in the Rue de Londres within sight of the great basilica of Sacré Coeur that had risen above Paris during the presidency of Marshal McMahon, and later in the Rue Gustave Doré. They were often seen together at the literary Fridays that took place at the *Chat Noir* café in nearby Montmartre – another meeting place for artistic Paris where the walls were covered with the paintings of such unfashionable artists as Gauguin and the Impressionists. Here she was often the butt of Debussy's jokes and by all accounts took them in good part so that it seemed the best kind of relationship for the sybarite composer.

Amongst the useful friends that Debussy made at this time was Edmond Bailly who ran the bookshop *Librairie de l'Art Indépendant* in the Chausée d'Antin, a centre for Symbolist ideas where the influential *Revue Indépendante* was published. Debussy made such a deep impression on Bailly that he gave him as much support as he could, saying to René Peter, 'This wonderful artist . . . will one day be the most famous of all.' Bailly introduced Debussy to many poets and artists including Pierre Louÿs, the photographer, poet and writer of risqué novels. He soon became one of the retiring composer's closest friends and it was in his home, where Debussy started to go almost every day, that the author Henri de Regnier observed the composer:

. . . with his flabby, nonchalant body, pale, matt complexion, vivacious black eyes under heavy, drooping lids, enormous, strangely indented forehead over which straggled a long lock of curly hair, and a general appearance of ardour and concentration, partly feline, partly gypsy . . . He was fond of books and precious objects, but always came back to music in the end, speaking little about himself, but judging harshly his contemporaries. The only ones to whom he showed any indulgence were Vincent d'Indy and Ernest Chausson. I don't remember anything striking about his conversation, but he spoke like an intelligent man, and held your interest, though his manner all the time was rather distant and evasive . . .

Le Chat Noir, 1885

Debussy also met the wealthy dilettante Étienne Dupin, who offered to take him to Bayreuth at his expense in 1888. The two heard *Parsifal* and *Die Meistersinger* on this visit which was repeated the following year when they heard *Tristan und Isolde*. These visits confirmed Debussy in his love of Wagner, but such was the semi-religious atmosphere of Bayreuth that he also began to see the danger of succumbing to such an overwhelming influence. The pseudo-Wagnerian operas appearing in Paris at the time confirmed how many talents were being swamped by 'the Old Wizard' as Debussy called Wagner with affectionate irony. Nevertheless, the desire to write an opera of his own surfaced and he reportedly told his old friend and mentor Guiraud after returning from Bayreuth that he wanted to set:

poems that will provide me with changing scenes, varied as regards place and atmosphere, in which the characters will not argue, but live their lives and work out their destinies.

We also find him continuing his old experiments with music by discovering the twelve-tone chromatic scale to replace major and minor – an avenue later to be explored exhaustively by Schoenberg and his followers. To Guiraud again he said: 'with them one can make any scale one wishes . . . [there are] ambiguous chords that belong to as many chords as one likes . . .' and he told other friends that he wanted to create a work in which,

Bayreuth

music would take over at the point at which words became powerless, with the one and only object of expressing that which nothing but music could express. For this, I need a text by a poet who, resorting to discreet suggestion rather than to full statement, will enable me to graft my dream upon his dream – who will give me plain human beings in a setting belonging to no particular period or country . . . Then I do not wish my music to drown the words, nor to delay the course of the action. I want no purely musical developments which are not called for inevitably by the text. In opera there is always too much singing. Music should be as swift and mobile as the words themselves . . .

What is clear from this is that Debussy had reacted strongly against the set aria and ensemble of traditional opera but could see the faults in Wagner's lengthy music dramas and had no wish to repeat them.

Whilst these musical projects were gestating in his mind and he reached out for his own original answers to their composition, he concentrated on less ambitious works: small-scale although charming salon piano pieces such as the two *Arabesques* of 1888 and the *Petite Suite* of 1889. He also composed his song cycle *Ariettes oubliées* (the second on poems by Verlaine to bear this title) and completed his three-movement *Fantaisie* for piano and orchestra – effectively a small-scale piano concerto. Having had no luck placing *La Damoiselle élue* with publishers, he sent it to the *Académie* as an *envoi* despite his no longer fulfilling the conditions of his association with that organisation. Their report on the work stated:

The text chosen is in prose and rather obscure, but the music is not deficient in either poetry or charm, although it still bears the mark of that systematic tendency towards vagueness of expression and form of which the Academy has already complained . . .

Another very important influence on his experiments came about in 1889-90 when Paris staged its *Exposition Universelle*. Debussy visited it with his friends the Swiss journalist Robert

The Annamite pavilion and the Central Colonial Palace, *Exposition universelle*, 1889

Godet and the composer Paul Dukas. The excitement this exhibition generated in the capital was electric. Rising above the large area known as the *Champs de Mars*, a steel structure unlike anything seen before had been constructed in less than a year as a tribute to French technical invention. The Eiffel Tower so dominated the landscape that its effect could only be compared with that of the first tower blocks to dominate European cities in the latter half of the twentieth century. That subtlest of short story writers, Guy de Maupassant, was so horrified by it that he actually ran away, hiding his eyes from its vulgarity, but to the visitors who rose in its lifts to see unrivalled views of Paris it was the very spirit of the Modern Age, that *Belle Epoque* that had seen such progress in the ordinary lives of human beings. Descending with their souvenir medals, they could visit the booths that huddled below, where almost every nation in the world including France's new colonies displayed its culture and products, vying with the sugar-cake pavilions where France's achievements were enshrined. It was in these booths and reconstructions of ethnic streets and market-places, rather than the more ponderous exhibits, that Debussy and his friends heard music such as they had never heard

The Annamite theatre,
Exposition universelle, 1889

before: not only genuine Hungarian gypsy music as opposed to the romanticised imitations beloved of the concert hall, but folk music from Europe, Africa, the Arab countries, Russia and, most fascinating of all to Debussy, the rhythmic Balinese and Annamite gamelan orchestras playing for the performance of shadow puppet plays and legendary dramas mimed by dancers in exotic and colourful costumes. Debussy wrote enthusiastically about his experience:

The people of Annam demonstrate the embryo of an opera in which the tetralogical formula can be recognised. Only there are more gods and less scenery. A small, ill-tempered clarinet directs the emotion. A tam-tam organises the terror . . . That is all.

The use of the pentatonic scale and the whole tone in this music was the primary revelation to Debussy and he particularly admired the economy of form that could reduce Wagner's conception of a tetralogy of operas to an afternoon's entertainment.

There was a festival of more traditionally exotic music as well. Of Russian music, Debussy heard Rimsky-Korsakov conducting works with which he was unfamiliar, despite his early visits to Russia. Such household names as Mussorgsky's *Night on the Bare Mountain*, music from Borodin's *Prince Igor* and Rimsky-

38

Korsakov's own *Caprice Espagnole*, with less familiar items, were a revelation to Paris. It was this that spurred Debussy into borrowing the score of Mussorgsky's opera *Boris Godunov* and he was to study it closely for nearly four years. What impressed him most was its declamatory speech-rhythms and the novel use of form, the music eschewing development for great set pieces and blocks of sound to achieve dramatic effect.

It was this continuous search for new influences and his attempts to incorporate them into his own music that kept Debussy a shadowy, Bohemian figure during these years, one full of maddening promise to his former teachers, but perverse in the direction that promise was taking. His few published piano pieces and songs did not extend his fame outside his own circle of acquaintances and the salons of a few wealthy hostesses, and he further retired from the limelight by antagonising the directors of the *Académie* who traditionally provided a concert to introduce the works of students returning from the Villa Medici. Although Debussy had left the Villa earlier than would normally be acceptable, they were willing to provide this concert in his case if he composed the usual overture and dropped his demands that the subversive *Printemps* be performed. Debussy refused to comply with either request, so the concert was cancelled.

A second chance to have a work performed at a *Société Nationale* concert conducted by Vincent d'Indy came to nothing later in the year through another extraordinary action by Debussy. His *Fantaisie* for piano and orchestra was scheduled – a work that, although minor Debussy, is no less accomplished than Fauré's famous *Ballade* for the same instruments – yet Debussy had misgivings about its slightness. Perhaps after voicing so many criticisms of contemporary composers he felt that such a work left him open to scorn so, after the public rehearsal, he collected all the parts from the music stands and vetoed any further performance. Left with a gap in his planned concert at such short notice, d'Indy was enraged and never entirely forgave Debussy, but the composer remained adamant and the work was never performed in his lifetime.

Debussy continued writing small-scale works, mostly for the piano. The Russian influence of the *Exposition* may be found in such pieces as the *Rêverie* and *Ballade* – originally entitled *Ballade Slav* – and his taste for the exquisite was gratified by a *de luxe* edition of his *Five Poems of Baudelaire* printed in a limited edition at Étienne Dupin's expense. Also from this period, although not published for another fifteen years, comes the *Suite bergamasque* for piano with its famous *Clair de lune* movement, testifying to Debussy's love of the *Commedia dell' Arte*.

At this time he also found a sympathetic publisher and friend in

Mussorgsky

Georges Hartmann whose interest in the publishing house Fromont ensured payment for, although often delayed publication of, many of Debussy's early works. He also advised him on money matters – never Debussy's strong point with his extravagant tastes – helped him find pupils for piano lessons and sent him a great deal of arrangement work, including two-piano reductions of Wagner and the then popular Raff. As well as this hackwork, Debussy also worked with Catulle Mendès, a colourful figure who lectured on Wagner with such passion that, according to Debussy, he frightened the ladies and their young daughters who came to hear him. Debussy played all the musical examples on a piano whilst these explosive diatribes continued and, recognising Mendès's influence and help, accepted a libretto from

Catulle Mendès

him based on the 'Cid' story which Massenet had also used for an opera then achieving such notable success in Paris. *Rodrique et Chimène*, as Mendès's version was called, was written in a distinctly Wagnerian dramatic style and, despite Mendès's exhortations to young French composers to find their own musical style based on folk song whilst utilising Wagner's dramatic methods, Debussy soon found that he was once more writing Wagnerian music.

Cramped by 'the Old Wizard of Bayreuth', Debussy was to labour at the work for two years, but only managed to complete two of the three acts. He wrote to a friend at the time: 'It is the exact opposite of everything I want to express . . . it demands a style of music that I am no longer able to write', and he vented his frustration by attacking Wagner in front of friends. One such outburst was recorded by the poet André Fontainas who witnessed it at Pierre Louÿs's house: Wagner apparently had elaborated Beethoven's worst traits – repetition for its own sake:

Do you believe that the same emotion can be expressed twice in a composition? . . . I should prefer the creation – and I shall do this myself – of a type of music that has neither motifs nor themes, or written on a theme that continues throughout without being interrupted or repeated . . . it will become more universal and psychic in its inspiration that way . . .

As relief from his labours on this impossible opera, his hackwork and private teaching, Debussy and Gaby would spend their spare time in the restaurants and cafés of Montmartre, where Debussy indulged his love of gourmet food and good wine. It was in one of these, the *Auberge du Clou* in 1891 that Debussy met Erik Satie, then employed as a cabaret pianist, and the two soon became firm friends.

The sympathy between these two utterly different men was to last until Debussy's death. In Satie, four years his junior, Debussy found an *alter ego* that pricked his own tendency towards the precious and the élitist. Most of Satie's music seemed to be written in order to mock pretentiousness: he used comic titles like *Bureaucratic Sonata* or *Three Pear-shaped Pieces*, and his love of the music hall and clowns touched a chord in Debussy as well, but he was also interested in those esoteric religious cults that were becoming fashionable at the time – Rosicrucianism, Spiritualism and Theosophy – and may have introduced Debussy to a cult sometimes known as The Priests of Zion, much involved with élitist transcendentalism. Certainly, Debussy's interest in the occult and in the mystical origins of musical composition become more apparent after his meeting with Satie. According to one person who met him in later life he regarded himself as a 'sensitive' tuned into a musical moment that has passed through time from infinity to infinity and, having passed through the composer, continues into a temporal distance. There are many such accounts of Debussy's mystical ideas and his notion of being in some ways a musical alchemist and magician; of more measurable importance however was Satie's influence in directing Debussy away still further from Wagner. Later Satie said:

Erik Satie, 1895

I explained the need every Frenchman has to free himself from the Wagnerian venture, which didn't respond to our natural aspirations. I also pointed out that I was in no way anti-Wagnerian but that we should have a music of our own – if possible without *Sauerkraut*. Why could we not use the means that Claude Monet, Cézanne, Toulouse-Lautrec and others had made known? Why could we not transpose these means into music? Nothing simpler . . .

In relation to opera, especially Wagner's use of the *Leitmotiv*, he said: 'There is no need for the orchestra to grimace every time a character comes onto the stage. Do the trees in the scenery grimace?'

The talks these two had together helped Debussy to clarify his musical ideas and, in 1892, when Debussy bought a copy of Maeterlinck's recently-published play *Pelléas et Mélisande* from a bookstall on the Boulevard des Italiens, he read it through at a sitting and realised immediately that this was the text he needed to bring his ideas to fruition.

The Belgian playwright and philosopher Maurice Maeterlinck was greatly interested in the power Fate has over individual lives and the shadowy, Medieval world of this play, although seemingly Wagnerian, treats this theme in a wholly Symbolist manner. In doing this, it avoids what Debussy had come to recognise as a certain Teutonic coarseness in Wagner's method – the *Sauerkraut* of Satie's phrase. But Debussy was not alone in his interest. The play acted like a magnet to musicians, all the more strange in that Maeterlinck himself was tone-deaf and did not understand music at all. Fauré was to write memorable incidental music for a London production of the play in 1898, and Sibelius wrote incidental music in 1905. Strangest of all, perhaps, in 1911 Arnold Schoenberg would produce a massive tone-poem based on the work, as a last tribute to his Expressionist period. Debussy, however, was the first and only one to see its operatic possibilities; consequently, he abandoned *Rodrigue et Chimène*, much to Mendès's anger, and immediately sketched some themes for *Pelléas et Mélisande*.

With this final rejection of Wagner, Debussy was now able to turn his attention to other projects which had been gestating in his mind. He began a *String Quartet*, possibly influenced by the vogue Beethoven's last quartets and the chamber works of Franck were having at that time in Paris. He also turned his attention to a poem by Mallarmé that had moved him with its evocation of the purely sensuous, *L'Après-midi d'un faune*. The original poem, which, as in all Mallarmé, aspired to the condition of music, was designed to be declaimed on stage – a not unusual entertainment at the time – and Debussy originally planned to write music to accompany this. He designed it in three parts: *Prélude*, *Interludes* and *Paraphrase finale* but he only completed the *Prélude*, and that would take him two years.

In April 1893, *La Damoiselle élue* was at last performed at a *Société Nationale* concert which also included music by Debussy's friends Dukas and Chausson. Its reception was favourable, especially amongst the followers of Franck, one of whom, d'Indy, forgetting Debussy's earlier slight for a moment, was so enthusiastic that Debussy suggested his praise 'would cause the

Detail from The Blessed
Damozel (*La Damoiselle
élue*) by Rossetti

lilies that lie asleep between the fingers of the Blessed Damozel to
blush'. Others were not so kind. The barbed critic of the *Echo de
Paris*, Henry Gauthier-Villars, otherwise known as 'Willy',
suggested it was 'a symphonic stained-glass window . . . more
fleur du mal than ever'. This neatly alluded to both the fading
vogue for Pre-Raphaelitism and the decadent climate of
Baudelaire's poetry. Bailly published it in a limited *de luxe* edition
with illustrations in suitably Pre-Raphaelite style, thus
emphasising the rarified atmosphere of the work.

In May, Debussy finally saw the play he had recognised as his
ideal libretto. *Pelléas et Mélisande* was performed at the *Théâtre des
Bouffes-Parisiens* to the almost total incomprehension of audience
and critics, but to the delight of Debussy who had his first feelings
confirmed on its suitability and set to work on the score with
renewed zeal. In September he wrote to Chausson, almost as an
afterthought: 'Latest News: C. A. Debussy finishes a scene of
Pelléas et Mélisande ("A Fountain in the Park" Act IV Scene iv) on
which he would like to have the opinion of E. Chausson', but
shortly afterwards he admitted that he 'tore the whole thing up'
because 'the ghost of old Klingsor, alias R. Wagner, appeared',
and he began writing the score all over again.

Although getting this far, he had still not received permission to use the text from Maeterlinck, so he arranged to go to Ghent and meet the author in his own home, setting off towards the end of the year with Pierre Louÿs for moral support. They stopped first in Brussels where they visited Ysaÿe. According to Debussy, writing again to Chausson, the great Belgian violinist hugged him and treated him like 'his little brother'. He continued:

That memorable evening I played in succession the *Five Poems of Baudelaire*, *La Damoiselle élue* and *Pelléas et Mélisande*. I got as hoarse as if I had been selling newspapers on the street   as for Ysaÿe, he became delirious.

After making this new friend, the two moved on. Debussy reported:

I saw Maeterlinck and spent a day with him in Ghent. At first he behaved like a girl meeting an eligible young man. Afterwards he thawed and became charming. He talked about the theatre as only a very remarkable man could. As regards *Pelléas*, he has given me full authorisation to make any cuts I wish, and has even pointed out some very important and very advisable ones. As far as music is concerned, he says he does not know a thing about it.

The friendship with Ysaÿe blossomed for, at the end of the year, Ysaÿe brought his quartet to Paris and included Debussy's new *String Quartet in D* in the concert they played at the *Société Nationale*. The audience, more used to Beethoven, Mozart,

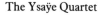
The Ysaÿe Quartet

44

Haydn and Franck at what were very élitist gatherings indeed, were utterly baffled by Debussy. Critics discovered memories of the gamelan or the 'influence of young Russia' and one found it 'bewildering, full of originality and charm . . . but diabolically difficult'. Even Chausson had misgivings about this original and lyrical work so that Debussy wrote to him: 'Well, I'll write another for you . . . and I'll try to bring more dignity in the form.' There is a great deal of insecurity in that statement for the work has entered the repertory, along with that of Ravel, his contemporary, who was greatly influenced by its novelty. Yet, although Debussy called it his *First Quartet, Op. 10* (the only work of his to bear an opus number), he never wrote the promised second.

Another performance was given by the Ysaÿe Quartet on 1 March 1894, in Brussels. The work that Debussy was also engaged on entitled *Prélude, Interlude and Paraphrase on l'après-midi d'un faune* was also announced, but Debussy was not happy with it and withdrew it for further revision. Instead he substituted *La Damoiselle élue* and some of his songs performed by a singer who had become a renowned interpreter of Debussy's music, Thérèse Roger. She had sung in the first performance of *La Damoiselle élue* and Debussy had become secretly engaged to her, although when Gaby found out a few months later there were scenes and the engagement was abruptly terminated.

The Brussels concert was generally well-received although some of the Belgian critics found the quartet 'oriental' and 'fantastic'. The influential Maurice Kufferath wrote: 'Is it music? Perhaps so, in the sense that the canvases of the neo-Japanese of Montmartre and its Belgian suburb may be called paintings.' He also declared that *La Damoiselle élue* had charm but contained much 'vagueness of expression'. All in all, he said, he had a 'curious impression of discomfort' during this concert 'as one feels on waking from a nightmare'.

Ignoring such criticism, Debussy continued to work. He produced his first set of *Images* for piano, but was dissatisfied with them, saying: 'These pieces would be terrified by the over-lit salons where there are people who don't really like music. They are like a discourse between the pianist and the piano.' They were not released in his lifetime with the exception of the middle movement, and only published in 1978 under the title *Images oubliées*. He also worked on *Pelléas et Mélisande* throughout 1894, but so fastidiously that it was to be at least another eight years before he was satisfied with it. He also discussed a fairy-tale opera with Pierre Louÿs to be called *Cendruline*, but kept changing his mind about the ideas and the libretto so that it came to nothing in the end, with Louÿs telling him in exasperation that he had better write the libretto himself.

Wrapped up in the world of *Pelléas et Mélisande* and the final version of his music for *L'Après-midi d'un faune*, Debussy, although physically in Paris, was far removed from the turbulent events that rocked the Third Republic that year: the assassination of President Carnot followed in a matter of months by the accession of two presidents and the condemnation of Captain Dreyfus as a traitor. This attack on a Jewish member of the armed forces was the anti-semitic corollary to several years of instability which had included an attempt to restore the monarchy, another attempt to unseat the republic by the charismatic General Boulanger, and the collapse of the Panama Canal Company which had ruined many people who then regarded it as a plot by Jewish financiers.

This treason trial which was soon to divide the whole nation left Debussy almost unmoved, although he had no sympathy with Dreyfus and his most ardent champion, Zola, whose realistic novels were totally against his refined aesthetic. Yet, although Debussy allied himself in conversation with the Nationalists who condemned Dreyfus, it was probably not for straight political reasons but a shrewd artistic choice. The case was to split France for another five years when Dreyfus was pardoned, and was to drag on until 1906 before he was declared completely guiltless. During that time salons were closed to members of opposing factions, the Dreyfusards faring the worse. Dreyfus supporters were attacked in the streets and at least one composer, Alfred Bruneau who knew Debussy, had an opera, *Messidor*, fail in the theatre in 1897 largely because he was a known Dreyfusard and had used a libretto by Zola. Zola himself had to escape to London to avoid prosecution after writing his pamphlet *J'accuse*.

Debussy's view of these events may be best seen through a letter he wrote to Pierre Louÿs.

I haven't got any further than you with the score of *Messidor* for life is short and I'd rather go to a café or look at pictures. How do you expect people as ugly as Zola and Bruneau to be capable of anything but the second-rate . . . with their social preoccupations and their claim to put life into chords of the seventh [they] are just a lot of dreary fatheads. If indeed they have any view of life at all, it is through their last laundry bill.

The *Prélude à l'après-midi d'un faune*, as it was finally called, shorn of its other two movements and thus dispensing with a narrator, could hardly have been further removed from these events and personalities. When it was at last performed at a *Société Nationale* concert on 22 December 1894, this serene, sensually pagan music, evoking as the programme note said, 'the successive scenes of the faun's desires and dreams on that hot afternoon' was so well received under Gustave Doret's direction that it had to be

LE FAVNE

Ces nymphes, je les veux perpétuer.

Si clair,
Leur incarnat léger, qu'il voltige dans l'air
Assoupi de sommeils touffus.

Aimai-je un rêve ?

Mon doute, amas de nuit ancienne, s'achève
En maint rameau subtil, qui, demeuré les vrais
Bois mêmes, prouve, hélas ! que bien seul je m'offrais
Pour triomphe la faute idéale de roses —

Réfléchissons...

ou si les femmes dont tu gloses

Nymphes from *l'Après-midi d'un faune*, illustrated by Manet

repeated. It was Debussy's first real success appearing on the programmes of other concerts shortly afterwards; and was to become in a brief period Debussy's first truly internationally performed work. This happened in spite of the critics who largely missed its extreme subtlety, the critic of *Le Ménestrel* saying it was:

finely and delicately orchestrated but one seeks in vain any heart or any strength. It is precious, subtle and indefinite in the same way as the work of M. Mallarmé.

Le Figaro said: 'It is amusing to write pieces like these, but they are nothing to a listener,' and another promised him a brilliant future if he returned to simplicity. Paul Dukas, however, saw its hidden strengths when he said: 'It is his ability to build a logical entity by using fantasy alone that puts M. Debussy's talents beyond comparison.' Debussy took up his pen in defence when he wrote to the influential 'Willy':

The *Prélude à l'après-midi d'un faune*, dear sir, is possibly the fragments of the dream lingering in the faun's flute. To be more precise, it is the overall impression of the poem, for if the music followed it too closely it would wheeze like a cab-horse racing a thoroughbred for the Grand Prix . . .

'Something about a faun in French,' declares Mrs Munt after a London concert in E. M. Forster's novel *Howards End*, 'which Helen went into ecstasies over, but I thought it most tinkling and superficial . . .' A neat summing up of the different attitudes this piece, that has been called the first truly modern score, continues to evoke.

The final word should lie with Mallarmé. He loved it when he heard it, and said that it had drawn out the emotion of his poem and gone even further, 'in nostalgia and in light, with delicacy, with uneasiness, with richness', and he wrote on a copy of the score:

> Sylvain d'haleine première
> Si la flute a réussi
> Ouïs toute la lumière
> Qu'y soufflera Debussy

(If the flute has played well, the primal woodland breath hears all the light that Debussy has inspired in it.)

At last, at the age of thirty-three, Debussy had sounded his real voice and become a name to be recognised. Typically, his fame had come quietly, in the refined and aristocratic tones of the *Prélude* rather than with some loud manifesto as would have befitted a Wagner or one of his coarser imitators. Revolutions, as Blake said, come on the feet of doves.

5 The Years of Pelléas

Although the *Prélude à l'après-midi d'un faune* had brought him briefly to the first rank of young French composers and he was now mentioned in the same breath as Dukas, Chausson, Duparc and their contemporaries, Debussy did not immediately follow up any opportunity this might have presented. Fastidious to the last, afraid to compose anything inferior to his new-found aesthetic, he was almost silenced by his success. 'How much one must create and then destroy whilst trying to touch the naked flesh of emotions,' he once wrote, and this explains the long periods his compositions took to write – the continual sketching and discarding of material that had produced only one short masterpiece in nearly twenty years. Such fastidiousness seemed the mark of several French composers – Dukas destroyed more works than he published, and Duparc is known chiefly for a handful of songs written in his early years – and it explains the slow progress Debussy made on *Pelléas et Mélisande* as he immersed himself deeper and deeper in the character and atmosphere of the play.

In one letter written to Chausson, who was his chief *confidant* during the writing of the opera, he revealed how close he was to his material at this time:

It's Mélisande's fault . . . I have spent days in pursuit of those fancies of which she is made . . . you know what such struggles are. I don't know if you have ever gone to bed, as I have, with a strange desire to cry, feeling as if you had not been able to see during the day some greatly loved friend.

The 'friend' so alluded to was Arkel, one of the more minor characters in the opera.

Although often seen at this time in his favourite haunts in Montmartre; in cafés and bookshops; at friends' houses where literature and art were discussed at length, or on picnics and outings to the woods around Paris, Debussy did not frequent musical circles by choice, and rarely performed in public. The rest of the time was spent in his 'little furnished flat in the Rue de Londres' as he described it, with Gaby in attendance, not always in blissful domesticity, as Debussy's eye continued to wander, and it was there that he painfully finished the first draft of what he knew would be his masterpiece.

He also worked on another original idea, inspired by Whistler's paintings and his meeting with Ysaÿe. He had written to Ysaÿe in September 1894:

I am working on three *Nocturnes* for violin and orchestra. The orchestra of the first part consists of strings; of the second, flutes, four horns, three trumpets and two harps; of the third, of both of these two groups. It is, in short, an experiment with the different combinations that can be obtained from one colour – like a study of grey in painting. I hope this will appeal to you . . . I am not forsaking *Pelléas* for this – and I must say that, the further I go, the more depressed and anxious I become . . .

Claude Debussy, Ernest Chausson, Raymond Bonheur and Mme Chausson by the Marne, 1893

To Henri Lerolle he had written in the previous month:

I have begun some pieces for violin and orchestra . . . in which I will employ groups of the orchestra separately, so as to try to discover nuances for these single groups . . .

Yet, even this project moved slowly and was to be greatly modified before being completed five years later.

Debussy finished his first version of *Pelléas et Mélisande* in the spring of 1895 and, when hearing of this, Maeterlinck wrote to the poet Camille Mauclair, who knew them both:

Sketch for *Pelléas et Mélisande* sent to Henri Lerolle in 1895

You know, I, unfortunately, am not only incompetent to judge, but that music is as unintelligible to me as if I were deaf . . . Do me the favour of going to listen to the score, and if you judge it good, I will authorise it.

Mauclair went with Pierre Louÿs to Debussy's flat where the composer played the score on his piano and sang all the parts. According to Mauclair's account, they:

went pale with emotion. When it was finished, Debussy said to me with his sarcastic smile: 'What are you going to say to M. Maeterlinck?' 'This,' I said . . . 'I have just heard one of the most beautiful masterpieces in all music, be proud and happy to have inspired it, send your authorisation immediately.'

Yet, when Mauclair asked Debussy where such an experimental work might be performed, he replied:

I do not know about that. I wrote it out of admiration for Monsieur Maeterlinck. It is no slight work. I should like to find a place for it, but you know that I am badly received everywhere. But I do hope that Robert de Montesquiou will be good enough to give two auditions at his Pavillon des Muses.

It is an indication of the rarified atmosphere which Debussy

Robert de Montesquiou by Whistler

knew his 'drame lyrique' (as he preferred to call it) inhabited, that he should have mentioned Count Robert de Montesquiou, even ironically. This rich dilettante was the central figure of *fin de siècle* Paris – a dandy and aesthete who, despite being mocked in Huysmans's *À Rebours* and, much later, the novels of Marcel Proust, was an intelligent patron of the arts, commissioning not only Whistler and his contemporaries, but the creator of exquisite glass, Emile Gallé, and the whole *Art Nouveau* movement that was emerging in France, filtering down through architecture even to the ornate entrances to the new Metro underground railway that ran beneath the streets of Paris. Montesquiou's Pavillon des Muses would not have been too ridiculous a place to stage Debussy's new work, but, a perfectionist to the last, he grew dissatisfied with the score. Prophetically, he had written earlier, 'God knows if it will not end in smoke' and, even now, he felt that it was too Wagnerian, writing to Chausson:

I felt the phantom of old Klingsor, the Wizard of Bayreuth and so I tore it all up and am now seeking for a more personal idiom and am trying to put in as much Pelléas as Mélisande. I have been pursuing music, trying to penetrate behind all the accumulation of veils by which she is shrouded from even her most ardent devotees, and I have brought back something which will please you perhaps! I don't care about anyone else. I have made use of a device which I think has been rarely used, namely silence (don't laugh!) as a means of expression – and perhaps the only way to give emotional value to a phrase . . . Ah! If only the times we were living in were less depressing, if only young people could be expected to take an interest in anything but the latest form of bicycle! Of course I've not the slightest intention of ruling over or shaping the tastes of my contemporaries, but, all the same, it would be nice to found a school of 'neo-musicians' where an effort would be made to preserve intact the admirably symbolic qualities of music . . . and the masses would be taught to show a little discrimination in their enthusiasm, so as to be able to distinguish, for example, between Franck and Massenet . . . The motto inscribed on public monuments [is to blame] 'Liberty, Equality, Fraternity' – words which at best are only fit for cab-drivers.

This typically Debussian railing against 'the masses' only reinforces the almost neurotic fear he had of writing even one commonplace or 'popular' bar. This feeling is communicated in the music which Saint-Saëns was eventually to call 'music on needle-points'.

Debussy did not tear up the first version of *Pelléas et Mélisande* as he told Chausson for its manuscript has been discovered, but he did go back to the beginning and rewrote almost every bar, putting in 'as much Pelléas as Mélisande'. This was to take another two years and such dedication was only made possible, given Debussy's extravagant lifestyle, through advances made by his publisher and friend Hartmann.

The Old Bridge at Battersea, London, by Whistler

The composer broke off from his revision of the work to visit London again in the summer of 1895, trying once more to get his music published there. He met Saint-Saëns on the channel crossing – not an unusual coincidence for the almost perpetually globe-trotting composer of *Samson et Delilah*. Although Saint-Saëns did not feel as enthusiastic about Debussy's music as Debussy did about his, they spent a congenial time together and Saint-Saëns introduced Debussy to several important English colleagues, also finding him lodgings with a French professor in Belsize Park. But Debussy found that the artistic climate in England had not improved since his previous visit – in fact, it had declined quite dramatically. He was present during the now infamous degradation of Oscar Wilde, who was sentenced to two years' hard labour for his homosexuality.

The fate of Oscar Wilde – that ostentatious flower of the English Aesthetic Movement which had so influenced Paris during Debussy's formative years – saw the beginning of a new philistinism. Verlaine was dying in London and, just as Debussy arrived there, many of the Aesthetes, mainstay of the 'Yellow Book', were throwing their green carnations away and heading for

Maurice Ravel

the more tolerant shores of France. English music was still presided over by the arch-Brahmsian Parry and the flippancies of Sullivan, so English publishers were in no mood to consider French music of any kind. Debussy's new and hard-won aestheticism seemed to be falling in ruins amidst the jeers of the newspapers and 'the masses' whom he loathed.

It could not have been a less auspicious time for the composer of *Prélude à l'après-midi d'un faune* to hawk his wares for, in many ways, it was the end of an era not only in England but also in Paris. George Moore, the Irish poet and novelist, who had lived on the fringe of the *décadent* movements in both Paris and London, wrote in 1893: 'Impossible to doubt any longer that the great French Renaissance of the beginning of the century has worn itself out, that the last leaves are falling, and that probably a long period of winter rest is preparing.' Yet such pessimism was the obituary of a movement only and, although a general feeling of decline associated with the end of all centuries was in the air, influences were only there to be assimilated for Debussy and their decline in fashion could not shake the firm foundations of his own creativity. He returned to Paris and continued to revise *Pélleas et Mélisande*.

During this time he was exposed to other influences. He became acquainted with the Spanish composer Albéniz – then studying at the Schola Cantorum with d'Indy and Dukas – and Maurice Ravel who, although thirteen years Debussy's junior and failing three times to win the *Prix de Rome* had nonetheless achieved a finished personal style. There were long conversations between the three, chiefly concerning piano technique which Albéniz possessed to a remarkable degree, but also including Spanish music. Both Debussy and Ravel fell under its sway and Ravel composed a *Habañera* for piano – performed as one of his *Sites Auriculaires* – that so interested Debussy that he borrowed it. Debussy's and Ravel's names are often linked but, apart from this period, they were never very close and soon drifted apart, although Debussy maintained his friendship with Albéniz for years afterwards. The *Habañera* was later to cause a rift between Debussy and Ravel, but Albéniz's piano technique inspired Debussy to begin a piece of his own – the three-movement suite *Pour le piano* which he wrote in 1896, although it was not to be performed until 1902. He also discussed various projects with Pierre Louÿs. Writing to Ysaÿe he said:

It is probable that by December I shall have finished a work I am doing on a poem by Rossetti – *La Saulaie* [a translation by Louÿs of *Willowwood*]. It is an important work and written in the light of my latest discoveries in musical chemistry.

But this, like the projected ballet on *Daphnis et Chloë* (later to be written by Ravel) and other vaguer projects, entered the same limbo as the ill-fated *Cendruline*. He did orchestrate two of Satie's *Gymnopédies*, which were performed in 1897, but throughout his friendship with Louÿs, he only completed one small chamber work in collaboration with him. This was the *Chansons de Bilitis*, based on pseudo-Greek erotic poems by the poet, which were originally designed to be declaimed against a delicate accompaniment of harps, flutes and a celesta. In this form it was given its only performance in Debussy's lifetime at the offices of the *Paris Journal*, although Debussy later arranged them as three songs for voice and piano. Even this was to dissatisfy him, however, as he later wrote to Louÿs: 'Really, what is the use of harmonising the voice of Bilitis in major and minor, since she is the possessor of the most pervasive voice in the world? . . . The music is for other occasions.'

By 1897, Debussy had finished his second draft of *Pelléas et Mélisande* and, despite being a highly-withdrawn composer known chiefly to his own small circle of friends and the salons of a few wealthy connoisseurs, he managed to place it with Albert Carré, the director of Paris's principal opera house, the *Opéra-Comique*. This was done mainly through the influence of André Messager, the conductor and composer of light ballet music who was a good friend of Debussy's. Yet, once more, Debussy procrastinated, calling the score back for further revision and, in the same mood of self-doubt that seemed to run through all his projects, apparently nearly destroyed it, only to be dissuaded by Louÿs. He recalled the score several times for further revision, especially after Carré had suggested that a concert performance may have been more appropriate for something as novel and intimate as *Pelléas et Mélisande*.

Carré should not be blamed for his lukewarm enthusiasm. Paris, although used to the mellifluous flow of a Massenet or a Gounod, still enjoyed its grand opera on a grand scale, with large set pieces among soaring recitatives, and arias which only the French language seems to fit like a glove. *Pelléas et Mélisande* has no 'set pieces', no grand ensembles, indeed, no 'arias' in the strict sense of the term, but maintains a lyrical flow of sound that is the exact counterpart of the words, only occasionally rising to 'melody' or 'dramatic action' when the dreamlike text demands it. This mirrors Debussy's search for 'a theme that continues throughout without being interrupted or repeated', as he had expressed it earlier in the company of his friends. Yet he could see that it was essentially a stage work when he wrote earlier to Ysaÿe, who had also wanted to arrange a concert performance:

If it has any merit, it is in the connection between the drama and the music. It is quite obvious that at a concert performance this connection

André Messager

would disappear and no-one could be blamed for seeing nothing in these eloquent 'silences' with which this work is starred. Moreover . . . the simplicity of the work only gains significance on the stage . . .

In 1896, when he wrote this letter, Debussy had also offered Ysaÿe his *Nocturnes* which were still cast in the form for violin and orchestra. Debussy is known to have been a great exaggerator in his letters, however, often telling friends that works were far more advanced than they really were, and it is doubtful whether the *Nocturnes* actually existed in the completed form he suggests in his letter to Ysaÿe, for the violinist never saw them and, shortly afterwards, Debussy recast them in a version for orchestra and women's chorus without solo violin.

Much of Debussy's uneasiness at this time must be traced back to his domestic affairs. He was having a relationship with a wealthy society woman, and Gaby found out. To Pierre Louÿs he wrote:

Gaby with her steely eyes found a letter in my pocket which left no doubt as to the advanced stage of a love affair with all the romantic trappings to move the most hardened heart. Whereupon tears, drama, a real revolver and a report in the *Petit Journal*. Ah, my dear fellow, why weren't you here to help me out of this nasty mess? It was all barbarous, useless and will change absolutely nothing. Kisses and caresses can't be effaced with an india-rubber. They might perhaps think of something like this and call it the Adulterer's India Rubber.

On top of it all, poor little Gaby lost her father – an occurrence which for the time being has straightened things out. I was, all the same, very upset.

Although things were 'straightened out' for the moment, the respite was only temporary for Debussy soon transferred his attentions to a friend of Gaby's, a dressmaker from Burgundy called Rosalie Texier. For a while, all three could be seen in each other's company at their favourite haunts, especially in the Brasserie Pousset with its Pre-Raphaelite décor. Debussy and his two women, with their friends Mendès, Messager, various writers and journalists and the fantastic poet Paul-Jean Toulet, who wanted to co-operate on a libretto with Debussy, must have been a striking sight. As one observer put it, Debussy had 'Assyrian' looks: black beard and curly hair, and looked so Pre-Raphaelite framed by the Medieval décor that one could see why the English likened his appearance to Dante Gabriel Rossetti when he had visited London, although his wide-shouldered, rather fleshy body seemed merely lazy. In this company, he might argue loudly or keep almost monastic silence depending on his mood; he would roll cigarettes with one hand, smoke heavily, and sip the 'English' beer or nibble at the finest delicacies as he did. After sampling as

La Brasserie Pousset, 1898

Claude and Lily Debussy,
c 1902

much as he needed of café society's endless quarrels, he would don his 'cowboy' style hat and voluminous cloak and leave with Gaby on one arm and Lily, as Rosalie became known, on the other.

This *ménage à trois* could not continue for long, however, and it was Gaby who was eventually ousted in 1898, Lily taking her place at the Rue de Londres. She was an immediate success with all Debussy's friends. Accounts say that she was an unaffected girl with brown hair and a pleasant, easy-going nature, practical, and a little delicate in appearance: 'She is unbelievably fair and pretty,' Debussy later wrote of her, 'like some character from an old legend.' Her only unattractive feature appeared to be her rather harsh voice which Debussy enjoyed mocking whenever he could. It is thought that Debussy offered to marry her almost immediately, but she refused the formal contract at first.

With his domestic affairs more harmonious, Debussy continued to work at *Pelléas et Mélisande* although his confidence on its progress could no longer be shared with Chausson, for his friend was killed in June 1899 in a cycling accident. He was only forty-four. That same year, Debussy also finished his *Nocturnes* in their new arrangement, then, after another of his dramatic suicide threats, Lily accepted his proposal of marriage and the two were married on 19 October with Pierre Louÿs and Erik Satie as witnesses. It is said that Debussy had to give a piano lesson in the morning to pay for the ceremony and reception, and that afterwards they all went to the circus, Debussy spending his last francs on a meal at the Brasserie Pousset later in the evening. Shortly afterwards, the couple moved to an apartment in the Rue Cardinet which was modest but large enough for Debussy to have a study which he had painted in his favourite green and decorated with Chinese silks and ornamental cats.

The old century died, and with it much of the 'decadence' that had been the hallmark of its artists. Oscar Wilde, newly released from prison, wandered around Paris cafés like a spectre of the *fin de siècle* for a few months, only to expire in 1900 at the seedy Hôtel d'Alsace. Debussy continued to visit his old haunts in Montmartre, but he began to find the poseurs tiresome, and at the elegant Chez Weber, where he would sit with a few friends, he observed the Paris *beau monde* sceptically: the Venezuelan musician and composer of salon music, Reynaldo Hahn, whom he especially hated for his influence and his vapidity together with his friend Marcel Proust, then regarded as an empty-headed socialite with no real connection with literature, bored him so much that when asked to their house, Debussy is supposed to have replied, 'But, you know, I am a real bear' and when they shared a taxi they did not exchange one word. Proust admired Debussy's music, and the composer is widely regarded as one of the models for Vinteuil in *À la Recherche du Temps Perdu*, but Debussy was perhaps worried by the edge of scandal the novelist skated so close to – he had had enough scandal of his own for the time being. The 'literary Fridays' at the Chat Noir still continued and Debussy could watch shadow plays performed in the top room there and see the latest paintings hung on every spare space on the walls, but the famous 'Tuesdays' at Mallarmé's flat had ceased with the poet's death two years earlier. The Brasserie Pousset and the Reynolds Bar where the cabaret clowns performed, continued to amuse him with the latest 'cakewalk' from America and the dancing of Mata Hari, but he was seen less and less. A new realism was abroad as hard-nosed as the new century would eventually become.

Marcel Proust

As Debussy worked on his Symbolist 'drame lyrique' in February 1900, the musical world was seduced by Charpentier's realistic opera *Louise*. Debussy saw it and hated it. In a letter to Louÿs he wrote:

It supplies only too well the need for that cheap beauty and idiotic art that has such an appeal . . . He has taken the cries of Paris that are so delightfully human and picturesque and . . . has tamed them into sickly cantilenas with harmonies underneath that, to be polite, we will call parasitic.

In this outburst, Debussy vented all his loathing of the realist school, led by Zola, that had turned such a harsh spotlight on the world. This was art for 'cab drivers' as Debussy wrote elsewhere, completely unlike his own subtle explorations of mood. He was equally scornful of that other 'New Wave' of realistic opera, the Italian *verismo* school as exemplified chiefly by Mascagni and Puccini's new *La Bohème* and was later to castigate its vulgarity as 'a film formula, whereby the characters fling themselves on each other and tear their melodies from each other's lips'. Because films at the turn of the century were crudely acted experiments in obvious effects, this opinion is doubly barbed.

More realism of the vulgar modern sort was inflicted on Paris by the *Exposition Universelle* that year. Unlike that of 1889 which had been such a powerful influence on Debussy, it contained little that was artistically stimulating but was marked by buildings of extraordinary ugliness including a Palace of Electricity and a ferris wheel which was to dominate the Champs de Mars for a further thirty years. The introduction of electric lighting in the streets of the capital and in certain wealthy homes that year was regarded by some as an additional intrusion on the character of the city, so that in an atmosphere of general banality, Debussy's *String Quartet*, *La Damoiselle élue*, and the *Chansons de Bilitis* in their new version for voice and piano performed at one of the concerts, must have seemed a highlight of taste. Recognition of his gifts appeared in a report written for the officials of the Ministry of Fine Arts by Alfred Bruneau in which he said that although '*L'après-midi d'un faune* is one of the most exquisite instrumental fantasies which the young French school has produced,' *La Damoiselle élue* was 'too exquisite, flabby and insipid', and for reasons connected with his own aestheticism, he thought *Louise* more important.

A more noticeable public achievement was the performance of the first two movements of the *Nocturnes* at the *Concerts Lamoureux* on 9 December 1900. On this occasion, Alfred Bruneau wrote of Debussy with unreserved admiration:

This musician, whose works are so rarely performed, is one of the most original and remarkable artistic personalities of the day. He is little known by the crowd, goes nowhere, composes, I fancy, only when he feels inclined, and lives like a recluse, scorning all noisy advertisement. What an admirable and rare example! . . . Having shut himself up, M. Debussy seems intent on expressing the transient impressions of the dream he is in quest of, rather than the eternal passions of the world which he shuns . . . The two pieces which we have just heard indicate that he continues in the same state of mind.

Shortly afterwards, Debussy dedicated this brilliant score to his wife:

This manuscript belongs to my little Lily-Lilo. All rights reserved. It is proof of the deep and passionate joy I have in being her husband. Claude Debussy. At the peep of January, 1901.

With his reputation growing, Debussy was offered the post of music critic to *La Revue Blanche* in April 1901. The journal had only a small readership, but it was an influential one and it was here that Debussy first showed his flair for pithy and apposite journalism. Taking the persona of a M. Croche, a 'Dilettante Hater', a 'spare, wizened man', he expressed his opinions on everything from the *Prix de Rome* to virtuosos and the opera:

60

'Have you noticed the hostility of a concert-room audience? Have you studied their almost drugged expression of boredom, indifference and stupidity?' M. Croche demands, and goes on to express Debussy's credo:

In all compositions I endeavour to fathom the diverse impulse inspiring them and their inner life. Is not this more interesting than the game of pulling them to pieces, like curious watches?

And again:

Discipline must be sought in freedom . . . Give ear to no man's counsel but listen to the wind that tells in passing the history of the world.

Concerning the national opera, of particular significance to his hopes for *Pelléas et Mélisande*, Debussy stated:

A stranger would take it for a railway station and, once inside, would mistake it for a Turkish bath . . . Music assumes the pompous proportions of the building, vying with the well-known great staircase which, through an error of perspective, or too much detail, in fact appears insignificant . . .

This did not matter, however, for the place was filled with *loges à salon* which were 'the most convenient places for not hearing anything of the music'. To the composer of *Pelléas et Mélisande*, an opera-going public made up largely of society people from the Jockey Club airing the latest fashions, and rooms where gentlemen seduced courtesans, must have seemed the most depressing experience of all, but though barbed and witty, his opinions carried little weight and in fact he soon regarded them merely as a source of extra income. In later years, however, he collected and arranged some of them for publication with later writings under the title 'M. Croche, the Dilettante Hater' – a book posthumously published.

After six months as music critic, he handed in his notice, finding the task of listening to other people's often indifferent music interfered with composition. Yet he managed to finish his first truly characteristic piano work, the suite *Pour le piano*, in 1901, and *Pelléas et Mélisande* was nearing completion, with its promise of a production at the *Opéra-Comique* the following year. Whilst working on these, he heard the first complete performance of the *Nocturnes* – the three movements *Nuages*, *Fêtes*, and *Sirènes* – on 27 October at the *Concerts Lamoureux*. It was received with great enthusiasm by audience and critics alike. The *Courrier Undine* wrote: 'One cannot imagine a more delightful Impressionist symphony. It is entirely made up of splashes of sound', and other papers were equally enthusiastic, one saying Debussy had achieved 'complete lucidity of thought and accuracy of expression'.

In a rare attempt to explain a work, Debussy had written a programme note:

The title *Nocturnes* is to be understood with a generalised and decorative meaning. So, we should not bother with the usual form a nocturne takes, but with its entire meaning by way of impressions and particular light effects. *Nuages*: this represents an unchanging view of sky, with a cloud procession that is melancholy and slow, but concluding with an anguished grey softly fading into a white tint. *Fêtes*: here there is the movement in the dance rhythm of the air, with sudden flashes of light. It also contains a procession episode which is a vision that is dazzling, but completely imaginary, that passes through the festival and intermingles; but the festival in the background blending music and luminous dust continues in a total rhythm. *Sirènes*: the sea and its countless rhythms, then the mysterious siren song is heard across waves turned silver with moonlight. It laughs and fades away.

Debussy, with these masterpieces behind him, and seemingly assured of a sympathetic hearing wherever his music was played, was at last persuaded to hand over the score of *Pelléas et Mélisande*. André Messager put it into rehearsal on 13 January 1902 and prepared to give this masterpiece to the world.

6 Success and Scandal

Maurice Maeterlinck

After spending ten years completing *Pelléas et Mélisande*, Debussy was to find the staging of the work a frustrating experience. The first problems centred on Maeterlinck. For some time, he had thought Maeterlinck's wife, the singer Georgette Leblanc, would sing the part of Mélisande and Debussy had even coached her at Maeterlinck's house, in his own apartment, and at rehearsals at the *Opéra*. 'He was always complimenting my enunciation, which gave him great pleasure,' she wrote later, but Albert Carré had taken a fancy to a young Scottish singer, Mary Garden, who had made a triumphant début in *Louise* a little earlier and could therefore be considered more of a box office draw. Debussy demurred and when he finally heard her sing the part, was so moved that he later confessed: 'That was the gentle voice that I had heard in my inmost being, with its hesitantly tender and captivating charm, such that I had barely dared to hope for.'

Maeterlinck did not learn of the substitution until he read about it in the papers. He was incensed at what he regarded as a betrayal and, not understanding the quality of the music, thought the best recourse would be to take out an injunction to prevent the playing of the work. He found he could not do this, so he set out to attack Debussy physically.

Georgette Leblanc's colourful account takes up the story:

Maeterlinck brandished his cane and announced to me that he was going to 'give Debussy a drubbing to teach him what was what' . . . This threat of a beating terrified me and I clung to Maeterlinck who jumped briskly out of the [ground floor] window . . . I did not picture Debussy with his tragic mask of a face taking kindly to a reprimand.

I watched the deserted street for Maeterlinck's return. Finally he appeared at the top of the hill, brandishing his cane to heaven with comic gestures.

The story was pitiable. As soon as he entered the *salon* he had threatened Debussy, who dropped into a chair while Mme Debussy distractedly ran towards her husband with a bottle of smelling salts. She had begged the poet to go away and, my word! there was nothing else to do.

Indeed, there was nothing as far as Maeterlinck was concerned, for *Pelléas et Mélisande* went into full rehearsal later in the month, Debussy having earlier deeply impressed the singers with his own performance at the piano in Messager's house. Messager records:

Debussy played his score . . . and sang all the roles in that deep sepulchral voice of his which often necessitated his transposing the parts an octave lower . . . The impression produced by his music that day was, I think, a unique experience. At first, there was an atmosphere of distrust and antagonism; then, gradually, the attention of the hearers was caught and held; little by little, emotion overcame them; and the last notes of Mélisande's death-scene fell amidst silence and tears. At the end, they were all quite carried away, and eager to set to work as soon as possible.

But Maeterlinck would not give up. There was talk of a duel, but this came to nothing. Instead, he wrote a letter published in *Le Figaro* on 14 April which disassociated him from the production, continuing, 'arbitrary and absurd cuts have made it incomprehensible', although he had in fact not only originally sanctioned them, but had edited some of the text himself. The letter continued:

. . . In a word, the *Pelléas* in question is a work that is strange and almost hostile to me; and deprived of all control over my work. I can only wish for its immediate and decided failure.

As if this was not enough, Debussy's benevolent publisher, Hartmann, had died, and General Bourgeat, who inherited the firm, demanded the return of the advances made to Debussy during the writing of the opera. Needless to say, Debussy could not repay them, so bailiffs were sent to issue court orders against the composer, who now found much of his time taken up with legal disputes.

When he could find the time, Debussy continued revising orchestration in the light of the rehearsals, and found he had to compose several orchestral interludes to cover the practical needs of the scene-shifters. Then, when the dress rehearsal did take place, there were outrageous scenes.

Someone, possibly Maeterlinck, had printed a 'select programme' which mocked the text, and this was sold outside the theatre. Inside, the trouble began during the second act: laughter, catcalls, and 'almost a riot' according to one paper. Debussy's friends and supporters rallied round and arguments continued loudly throughout the rest of the performance. Afterwards, Debussy was forced to cut one scene and the official censor demanded that a section which mentioned the word 'bed' should be removed as offensive to propriety.

At the first official performance, although many of the people Debussy had railed against were there – society subscribers who went to be seen and not to listen – an enthusiastic group of students who had heard of this novel new work filled the cheaper seats and applauded wildly, shouting down any attempts at criticism.

From then on, the work had a quieter passage in the opera house, but many critics took up the catcalls of the audience. One described the music as 'like the noise of a squeaky door or a piece of furniture being moved about, or a child crying in the distance', others, generally, that it 'lacked melody', by which they meant the grand arias and ensembles that Debussy had deliberately tried to avoid; that it was 'invertebrate' or, as a former fellow-student of Debussy wrote, no doubt remembering with bitterness the harangues Debussy had made against the music of his time and their own spinelessness in accepting it: 'Art of this kind is morbid and pernicious . . . The germs it contains are not those of life and progress, but of decadence and death.'

There were many, however, who recognised the great

Pelléas et Mélisande (Act I, scene 3) at the *Opéra-Comique* in 1902. Mary Garden as Mélisande

Pelléas et Mélisande at the
Opéra-Comique in 1902.
Jean Périer as Pelléas

originality and beauty of the score, among them, Debussy's friends Pierre Lalo – son of Eduard Lalo – Dukas, and even d'Indy, who all wrote enthusiastically as well as lesser-known critics such as André Corneau, who said in *Le Matin*:

A work of art original in its impression, and subtle in expression; one is overjoyed to find no imitation of Wagner, Gounod or Massenet . . . One is overcome by the haunting sorcery and the subtle intoxication of this music.

Another critic noticed the influence of Mussorgsky, although this, it must be said, could only be detected in Debussy's use of declamation and natural speech rhythms. Another said, 'M. Debussy takes his place, more definitely even than Wagner, amongst the sensualists in music, of whom Mozart was the greatest', whereas Romain Rolland said it was 'one of the three or four outstanding achievements in French musical history'. Even d'Indy was enchanted, saying: 'Many-coloured waves of music . . . reveal hidden meanings . . . while always permitting the words to be discernible through the fluid element of the music.'

When asked his own opinion of the score, Debussy modestly replied:

I have tried to obey the law of beauty which seems to be singularly ignored when dealing with dramatic music. The characters in this drama endeavour to sing like real persons . . . I do not pretend to have discovered anything in *Pelléas*, but I have tried to mark out a path which others may follow and make broader with their own discoveries, in such a way, perhaps, as to liberate dramatic music from the heavy yoke it has been wearing for so long.

The opera continued to go from strength to strength during the fourteen performances it had that summer. Debussy was lucky to have such sympathetic interpreters. To Messager, the conductor who had nurtured the work throughout its creation, Debussy wrote: 'Each impression in *Pelléas* was doubled by what your personal emotion had found in it and had given it thereby a marvellous sense of appropriateness', so he dedicated the score to Messager, and in memory of Hartmann. Yet he was also overjoyed with the box office takings and his own royalties: 'that's what counts,' he said.

Discriminating audiences packed the house that summer when *Pelléas et Mélisande* alternated with Eduard Lalo's *Le Roi d'Ys*. The controversy the work had caused was now transformed into a style for which Debussy felt little sympathy. His more ardent admirers, according to a humorous article by Jean Lorrain, were *Pelléastres* or Debussyists – highly-strung devotees of a new cult who appeared to worship in a certain mode:

66

. . . that fair-haired girl, too frail, too pale, too fair, who has evidently got herself up to look like Miss Garden . . . that group of good-looking young men (nearly all the Debussyists are young, very young) whose long hair is skilfully brushed across their foreheads, those youths with the plump, pallid faces, deep-set eyes, velvet-coloured coats, slightly puffed sleeves, frock coats a little too tight at the waists, wide satin cravats that thicken their necks, or floating *lavallière* ties . . . The initiated greeted one another in the corridors, finger on lips; peculiar handshakes were hastily given in the semi-darkness of the boxes; their faces wore a tortured expression and eyes a faraway look . . .

Yet despite the reputation that a few writers created for the work as being reminiscent of a disease or the quasi-religious rites of Bayreuth, the opera was to be hardly ever out of the repertoire during Debussy's lifetime and remains to this day a unique masterpiece that receives constant revivals. With this one work Debussy liberated French opera from the pervasive influence of Wagner, an influence that had blighted Magnard's career, and produced such derivative works as Chabrier's *Gwendoline*, d'Indy's *Fervaal* and Chausson's *Le Roi Arthus* – works that had, with many others by their contemporaries, caused Paris to be dubbed 'little Bayreuth', and of which Debussy wrote:

We are bound to admit that nothing was ever more dreary than the neo-Wagnerian school in which the French genius had lost its way among the sham Wotans in Hessian boots and the Tristans in velvet jackets.

Pelléas et Mélisande made Debussy famous overnight. The French government presented him with the *Croix d'Honneur* which he accepted 'for the joy it will give my old parents', as he told Pierre Louÿs, but the public acclaim mingled with abuse and the following of a clique irritated Debussy, who was by now worn out. He wrote to Godet that, because of the trouble he had had to undergo, he thought he was suffering from the

Mary Garden: cartoon by Luc

fashionable neurasthenia . . . What I foresee is that I shall continually be pushed into public life. I am not really made for that kind of thing and all I shall be is my clumsy self.

To escape from Paris, he went to spend the summer with Lily at her parents' house in Bichain, and the modest stationmaster's home was exactly the right retreat for his shattered nerves. Here he began work on a libretto of his own for a projected second opera based on Edgar Allan Poe's story *The Devil in the Belfry*. In this he envisaged the chorus as the only singing part and the Devil as a character who would whistle, but not sing, as he made fools of a group of provincials. It was to occupy him as an idea for many years. He wrote to Messager:

The Devil is represented as cynical and cruel – much more devilish than the red, brimstone-breathing clown that has, so illogically, become a tradition with us. I should also like to put an end to the idea that the Devil is the spirit of evil. He is simply the spirit of contradiction; perhaps it is he who inspires those who do not think like everybody else.

Later, explaining his curious 'experiments' with this opera, he wrote:

As for those people who are kind enough to hope that I shall never escape from *Pelléas*, they are very much mistaken. Surely they must realise that if such a thing were to happen I should immediately devote myself to the cultivation of pineapples for I think it is quite disastrous to repeat oneself.

He also discussed a setting of Shakespeare's *As You Like It* with the poet Paul-Jean Toulet, who would have written the libretto but was addicted to opium, which made him too lazy, and left shortly afterwards as a colonial official to the new French colony of Tonkin. Debussy wrote to him there:

I am frightened to have you leave so soon. You have made me impatient to get in hand the complete scheme of this human little fairy play.

Other projects that interested Debussy at the time included operas based on Don Juan, and the Orpheus myth, but nothing came of these. In the autumn, he returned to Paris where he was once more involved in productions of *Pelléas et Mélisande*, complaining bitterly that it was deadening his sensibilities. He did manage to compose piano music, however: the slight *D'un cahier d'esquisses* and the more substantial *Estampes*, or 'etchings' which used Spanish rhythms, contained a portrait of the pagodas he had seen at the two *Expositions Universelles* plus experiments with the whole-tone scale and the soft pedal in his first truly characteristic manner. He also received a commission from a Mrs Eliza Hall of Boston to write a rhapsody for saxophone and orchestra. She had been advised by her doctor to take up this instrument to improve her failing hearing, and was commissioning works from various composers of the time including d'Indy, who wrote a *Choral Varié* for her. When Debussy saw her play this work at a later date, she was wearing a pink dress. This did not inspire Debussy, who hated writing to order and thought the lady's concert appearance, with her ungainly, and then quite novel instrument, absurd. Nevertheless, he had accepted the money, and continued to sketch the odd few bars half-heartedly.

At the beginning of 1903 he also resumed his journalistic career for a few months, this time with the small journal *Gil Blas*. Once more, the barbed wit flowed. Of Felix Weingartner conducting

The Wave by Hokusai, illustrating the cover of *La Mer*

Beethoven's *Pastoral Symphony* at a Sunday afternoon *Lamoureux* concert he wrote:

> He . . . conducted the *Pastoral Symphony* with the care of a conscientious gardener. He tidied it so neatly as to produce the illusion of a meticulously finished landscape in which the gently undulating hills are made of plush at ten francs the yard, and the foliage is crimped with curling tongs.

In April, he visited London once more, in order to review *The Ring* conducted by Hans Richter at Covent Garden. He greatly admired the English opera house, then employing his friend and champion Messager as artistic director, and he compared it favourably with Paris:

69

It is not for me to say precisely in what the superiority of the Anglo-Saxons consists but, amongst other things, they have Covent Garden . . . More attention is given to perfect acoustics than to sumptuous decorations, and the orchestra is numerous and well-disciplined.

After the four-night marathon of *The Ring*, Debussy relaxed by visiting one of the music halls that were London's speciality and whose brand of raucous humour he enjoyed as an antidote to too much culture. Debussy, although often an élitist when he considered his own art, recognised fully the vital energy of the people's culture.

He gave up the post of critic in June and left with Lily to spend the summer once more in Bichain. Here, the musical evocations of the sea, which appear as episodes in *Pelléas et Mélisande*, crystalised into a full-scale idea. Perhaps his recent channel crossing had something to do with stirring memories of the sea, but he was seen writing to Messager:

I am working on three symphonic sketches entitled: (1) *Mer belle aux Îles sanguinaires*; (2) *Jeux de vagues*; (3) *Le vent fait danser la mer* – under the general title of *La Mer*. Perhaps you don't know that I was originally intended for a sailor's career, and that only life's vicissitudes drew me away from that. I still have a real passion for it, however. I expect you will say that the hills of Burgundy aren't washed by the sea and that what I'm doing is like painting a landscape in a studio, but my memories are endless and are in my opinion worth more than the real thing which tends to pull down one's ideas too much.

This was the first reference to his symphonic sketches *La Mer*, and it is interesting to note that this most realistic sound portrait of the sea should have been not only inspired by memories, but by a highly stylised painting of the sea by the Japanese artist Hokusai whom Debussy greatly admired. This painting was later used, at Debussy's suggestion, to illustrate the cover of the published score, yet the symbolic meaning of the sea is shown in Debussy's letter written later to his publisher Durand:

In nature it is the real thing that restores us best. Yet people don't respect the sea enough . . . Bodies deformed by ordinary life should not be allowed to bathe in it, it is enough to make the fish weep. There should only be sirens in the sea . . .

In these musings on the sea, there is no hint of the emotional problems that were troubling the Debussys at this time: everything seemed calm on the surface, but there were disturbing undercurrents. Friends who visited them in Paris at the end of 1903 and the beginning of 1904 were aware only of domestic comfort, but Debussy had been tiring of Lily for some time. He secretly admitted that her voice grated on his nerves; he had not been faithful to her; the couple were childless; Debussy confided that he wanted children, and the problem of money was unresolved, despite increased revenues from the performance and publication of his works. In order to alleviate his financial difficulties he still gave private lessons, and it was this which led to a meeting in 1904 which was to change his life dramatically once again.

7 More Scandal

1904 began badly enough when, after Ricardo Viñes, the renowned interpreter of Debussy's works, gave the first performance of *Estampes* at the *Société Nationale*, Ravel noticed a disturbing similarity between the *Habañera* he had lent Debussy and the second movement of the new work, *Soirée dans Grenade*. Although Albéniz called Debussy's music a perfect evocation of Spain and the 'moonlit waters near the Alhambra', Ravel was outraged and began a public scandal.

Debussy was often careless about the odd influence on his music – there are similarities between Mussorgsky and parts of the hated *Louise* in his *Nocturnes* and the finger may be pointed at other 'borrowings', although never to the charge of outright plagiarism. He might have quoted Wilde's remark about seeing a flower with three petals and wishing to give it four, but instead he utterly denied Ravel's accusations, saying that he had mislaid Ravel's original manuscript without even realising it, which irritated the fastidious Ravel even more. The scandal came to nothing worse than bad feeling, but when Ravel published his *Rapsodie Espagnole* some years later, including the orchestrated *Habañera*, he was careful to add the date of its original composition.

More serious complications occurred when, after giving a piano lesson to Raoul Bardac, the boy introduced Debussy to his mother, Emma Bardac, the Jewish wife of a wealthy banker and a woman whose voice Debussy had admired for some time when she sang the *mélodies* of Fauré, Duparc and their contemporaries at the salons of her wealthy friends. One account records that they went for a drive in her carriage along the Bois de Boulogne and that Debussy, in the style of many a French novel of the period, proposed an affair in these romantic circumstances. Whatever the beginnings, their relationship blossomed and Debussy finally decided to leave Lily. He went to spend the summer with Mme Bardac in Jersey and it was there that, in the full flush of his new love, he wrote the piano pieces *Masques* and *L'Île joyeuse*, both inspired by the eighteenth-century artist Watteau, whose painting, *The Embarkation for Cythera*, showing masked lovers leaving for Aphrodite's island of love, provided a symbolic counterpart to Debussy's own lovers' flight to an island.

On his return to Paris, he told Lily frankly that he was leaving her for Emma Bardac. There was a tremendous scene, and, as in the parting from Gaby, a revolver was produced. This time, however, the jilted woman pointed it at her own breast and fired.

She was admitted to hospital where, it appears, Debussy did not even visit her, let alone pay the hospital bills, as she lay close to death. There was a huge scandal with every newspaper featuring the event, for Debussy was now the famous composer of *Pelléas et Mélisande*. Lily slowly recovered, but her hospital bills could not be met. Most of Debussy's friends looked unfavourably on him, thinking that he had behaved callously towards Lily, leaving her for a rich society woman. She was very popular with them, and they collected money amongst themselves to help her, many, including Pierre Louÿs, openly quarrelling with Debussy. Musical colleagues also regarded him with distaste, Fauré refusing to speak to him, although for slightly more personal reasons. He had been involved with Emma Bardac himself as early as 1892, and had even dedicated his song cycle *La Bonne Chanson* to her. Altogether, it seemed a disastrous move on Debussy's part.

Debussy wrote to Messager in September:

My life during the last few months has been strange and bizarre, much more so than I could have wished. It is not easy to give you particulars, it would be rather embarrassing . . . I have had many a fall, and have hurt myself so much that I have felt utterly exhausted for hours afterwards . . . I have been mourning the Claude Debussy who worked so joyfully on *Pelléas*; for, between ourselves, I have not be able to recapture him, and that is one of my many sorrows.

Yet, even with these trials, one should not forget Lily. Debussy had once loved her and had even put her into a play on which he collaborated with René Peter, *Les Frères en Art*. There he said of her: 'You don't pretend to be a muse who frightens the sparrows away. You don't do your hair like the women in the frescoes. You have a lovely perfume and you are as sweet as a peach . . .' In many ways she never recovered from this treatment and it is hard not to blame Debussy in some measure for this.

Despite being 'utterly exhausted', Debussy nevertheless managed to do some work. Apart from the two piano pieces already mentioned, he wrote a reasonable amount of music that year: the *Danse sacrée et danse profane* for harp and orchestra, commissioned by the firm of Pleyel to show off a new chromatic harp; the *Trois Chansons de France*, based on poems by Charles d'Orleans; and a second set of *Fêtes galantes*, both works dedicated to Emma 'my little darling, to thank her'. He also composed two pieces of incidental music commissioned by the well-known impresario Antoine for a production of *King Lear* at the Odeon Theatre although 'my family tribulations', as Debussy called his abandonment of Lily, prevented him finishing the project and they were never performed. When he could, he continued work on *La Mer* and Mrs Hall also appeared to claim her saxophone piece. Debussy wrote:

Having accepted that this Rhapsody has been commissioned, paid for, and eaten for more than a year, it would seem that I am somewhat behindhand with it.

and again:

The Americans are proverbially tenacious. The saxophone lady has landed in Paris . . . and is inquiring about her piece . . . So here I am searching desperately for novel combinations calculated to show off this aquatic instrument . . . I have been working as hard as in the good old days of *Pelléas*.

Yet despite these, and other tenacious demands from the good lady, Debussy never completed the work. It was later completed and orchestrated by Debussy's colleague Roger-Ducasse, and, as far as is known, Mrs Hall never performed it either with or without the pink dress that had so embarrassed Debussy.

All these commissions accepted by a composer who hated writing to order show the real financial problems that Debussy was undergoing, despite supposedly running away with a rich woman. He needed all his money when the scandal over his love-life took a turn for the worse and both Lily's and Emma's husbands sued for divorce from their respective spouses. Although Sigismond Bardac had abandoned Emma for an actress, the cases were not open and shut and were to drag on through the courts for another year. Debussy eventually wrote that he 'was finally only allowed to think by permission of the [court] usher'. When Debussy's music was performed, it seemed to draw especially bad notices, possibly for reasons other than the purely musical. The *Danse sacrée et danse profane* were first publicly performed in November at one of the *Concerts Colonne*. The *Guide Musicale* wrote of this transparently beautiful work: 'In M. Debussy's music dissonance has become the rule . . . it is vague, hazy, disturbing, almost morbid', and the writer went on once more to rail against 'Impressionism' – this was now a rather old-fashioned term of abuse for the movement had broken up with bitter exchanges between the surviving Impressionist painters. It had largely been superseded by the Symbolism of Gustave Moreau, Odilon Redon and the early Expressionists whom Debussy now admired and, although Cézanne was painting his famous *Grandes Baigneuses* in 1905, it was also the year when the Fauve group was formed by Matisse and Derain.

A further performance by Viñes of *L'Ile joyeuse* and *Masques* in February 1905 brought more gratifying, if grudgingly appreciative reviews, but Paris was soon unbearable for Emma and Debussy, so they left their new apartment in the Avenue Alphaud that spring and escaped to England via Jersey. Before leaving, he had written to one new friend. The critic Louis Laloy learned:

You should know how many people have deserted me. It is enough to make one sick of everyone called man. I shan't tell you everything I have gone through. It's ugly and tragic and ironically reminds me of a novel a concierge might read. Morally, I have suffered terribly. Have I some forgotten debt to pay to life? I don't know, but I've often had to smile so that no one should see that I was going to cry.

In Jersey, Debussy took up *La Mer* once more. He wrote to his new publisher, Jacques Durand from there: 'The sea has been very good to me, she has shown me all her moods.' Durand was one of Debussy's few strokes of good fortune that year. The publishing house had originally given him hackwork in his early freelance days, and now it offered him a monthly income in respect of royalties that would accrue from future works. Debussy needed this money. In August he heard that Lily's divorce had been granted, with alimony to be paid to her by him from the royalties of certain works.

That same August the couple moved on. Debussy wrote to Laloy of 'several days spent in London without much joy, except for the music of the grenadiers who used to pass every morning with their joyful bagpipes and the wild little fifes playing marches in which the Scotch song seemed to melt into the cakewalk.' Debussy noted this tune down and was to use it four years later in his *Children's Corner Suite* for piano.

Children were much on Debussy's mind at this time for Emma was pregnant with the child he had longed for and which Lily could not give him. They moved on to Eastbourne on the South Coast where once more he wrote to Laloy:

I've been here a month. It's a little English seaside place, silly as these places sometimes are. I shall have to go because there are too many draughts and too much music – but I don't know where . . . I have written a certain amount of music as I have not done for quite a time.

Despite the music he heard (mostly distracting arrangements

Claude and Emma Debussy,
Bois de Boulogne

for brass of Sullivan, Edward German, and military marches played in seafront bandstands) he finished the orchestration of *La Mer* whilst overlooking the sea from the windows of the Grand Hotel.

They were back in Paris in October when Emma gave birth to a daughter, called Claude-Emma but nick-named Chou-Chou. Shortly after this, Emma's divorce was granted with substantial alimony from her rich ex-husband, and Debussy married Emma. The Debussys could now afford to move to a house with a garden on the Bois de Boulogne with its fashionable promenades and restaurants. Here Debussy could expand and indulge in those luxuries he had always regarded almost as a right. Here, too, he could keep a cat – the animal to whom he was most often likened. She was a grey Angora called Line, the first of several of that breed all of whom bore the same name. Their new sense of wealth and security did not last long, however, for Emma's alimony was only paid for a short time, requiring further legal battles to be fought, and eventually all Debussy's old money problems returned.

In October the long-awaited performance of *La Mer* took place at the *Concerts Lamoureux* under Camille Chevillard. By all accounts, it was an indifferent reading, as Chevillard did not understand the novelty of the score. Many people were duly disappointed. Pierre Lalo, who had fallen out with Debussy over Lily, recalled the sea music in *Pelléas et Mélisande* which he considered superior:

It seems to me that in *La Mer* the sensibility is neither as intense nor so spontaneous; I think that Debussy desired to feel, rather than actually felt, a deep and natural emotion. For the first time in listening to a descriptive work of Debussy's I have the impression of beholding not Nature, but a reproduction of Nature, marvellously subtle, ingenious and skilful, no doubt, but a reproduction for all that . . . I neither hear, nor see, nor feel the sea.

Other critics were bemused by the subtitle 'Three Symphonic Sketches' which Debussy had chosen to avoid comparison with the three-movement French symphony of the time developed by Franck, Chausson and others. To them, it was a rigorously logical

Manuscript of *La Mer*

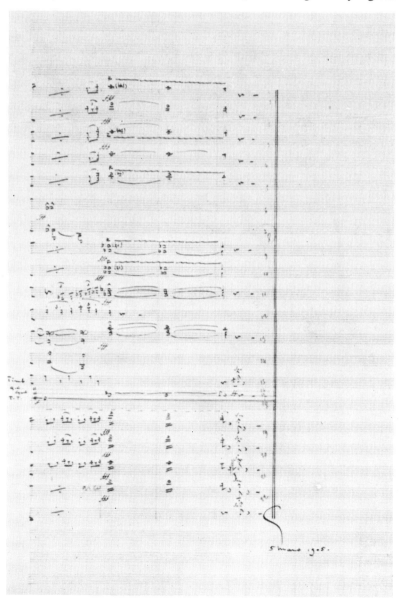

symphony, and not 'programme music' at all, although one, M. D. Calvocoressi, who was later to become a friend and champion of the composer, saw: 'a new phase in M. Debussy's evolution . . . One has the impression that M. Debussy . . . has here considerably condensed and clarified the sum total of his discoveries.'

With such animosities aroused, Debussy was hardly given a fair hearing and *La Mer* had to wait at least three years before it was acknowledged to be the masterpiece it truly is. His second marriage marked a watershed in his life, however, and from then on his bohemian days were definitely over.

8 The Family Man

Gradually, the fuss surrounding Debussy subsided and animosities ceased to be openly voiced as he distanced himself completely from both enemies and followers alike. The latter, the *débussystes*, formed a noisy *claque*, imitating Debussy's unusual hats and arguing loudly in favour of his music at public performances. Debussy complained 'The *débussystes*, are killing me.'

In his cosy home, the family man indulged his increasing desire for seclusion. He was no longer seen in the fashionable cafés and restaurants of his bohemian days and began to formulate ideas of a mystical withdrawal into music. He wrote in a letter:

Music should have been an hermetical science enshrined in books so difficult to understand that it would discourage all those herds of people who regard it with the same casual attitude that they would a handkerchief . . . Rather than encouraging the people to appreciate music I propose founding a Society for Esoteric Music.

At the same time, he regarded himself almost as an alchemist when composing; to him, it was akin to a magical act to bring such bewitching sounds as his out of silence, and he talked more often of his 'latest experiments in musical chemistry'.

In 1905 he wrote the first of his two books of *Images* for piano, a set written in 1894 having remained unpublished. In these, he continued to experiment by producing an evocation of reflections in water as well as an esoteric homage to the early eighteenth-century composer Rameau, one of whose operas he was revising at the time, and it is in these pieces that his use of the whole-tone scale to avoid major and minor tonality was at last consolidated. When Debussy sent this first set to Durand that same year he wrote prophetically:

I think I would say without due pride that I believe these three pieces will live and take their place in piano literature . . . either to the left of Schumann . . . or the right of Chopin.

Ricardo Viñes

They were first performed by Ricardo Viñes on 3 March 1906 at a *Société Nationale* concert and achieved notable success. This was one of the few original works to be made public that year although, due to public demand which began to take interest in the composer of *Pelléas et Mélisande* once more, some publishers who had secured rights on Debussy's early works during the period of his deeper financial troubles began reissuing them under new titles. Two orchestral interludes from *L'Enfant prodigue* were published in addition to his early *Danse styrienne* and a song orchestrated by another hand *Jet d'eau*. This led to charges that Debussy had written himself out and that he was offering 'warmed-up fare'. Debussy did not sanction these versions, but had no control over them any longer. All he could do was write to his publisher Durand when hearing that the *Cortège et Danse* from *L'Enfant prodigue* was to be performed at a concert conducted by Colonne that they were 'hardly interesting enough' after *La Mer*, the *Nocturnes* and *Images*, 'I should be afraid that people would accuse me of dragging out all my old compositions in order to keep my name consistently on the concert posters.'

One of the ever-vigilant critics, Emile Vuillermoz, wrote:

One wonders whether, during his long periods of idleness, M. Debussy is losing that marvellous skill . . . which had made him one of the most remarkable poets of the modern orchestra . . . Let the composer of *Pelléas* read the works of the young composers who are regarded as his pupils . . . There, very skilfully treated, he will find all the new sonorous effects which he seems to have forgotten.

Claude-Emma Debussy (Chou-Chou) as a baby, 1906

Yet, despite these jibes, and personal tragedy – his father had died in 1906 – he had been working hard. Inspired by his family and especially his daughter – Chou-Chou's nursery and her first attempts to walk – he began a new suite of piano pieces, a tribute of love from the family man which would eventually be called *Children's Corner*. He also toyed once more with the sketches for his opera *The Devil in the Belfry*, but put these aside soon afterwards in favour of a new project, *Tristan et Yseult*. This was to be an opera based on troubadour songs and episodes and was to be as French as Wagner's *Tristan* was Teutonic – another example of Debussy's desire not to repeat *Pelléas et Mélisande*. During 1907 he worked on its libretto with the poet Gabriel Mourey, a translator of Swinburne and Poe, and such was public interest that a musical magazine announced it was finished and would be performed at the *Opéra-Comique* the following year. Debussy sent a letter that August to his publisher including 'one of the 363 themes' from the projected work but, despite all this enthusiasm, nothing came of it.

He also began work on a second and third set of *Images*. The second set, originally for two pianos, slowly transformed themselves into an orchestral work in which Debussy would pay tribute to England, France and Spain; but the third set, conceived totally for piano was published in 1907 as the Second Set, a companion to the set for piano written in 1905. In his latest set he continued his experiments with piano technique, exploring pictorial 'Impressionistic' moods. He wrote this music on three staves instead of the usual two in an attempt to capture even more rarified sounds: bells heard through leaves inspired by a letter of Louis Laloy's in which he described bells heard at Hallowe'en through a forest, and a ruined temple, the title also suggested by Laloy who described the piece as 'like a translucid precious stone born of space and silence'. Inspired by a piece of Chinese lacquerwork in Debussy's study, the other movement describes goldfish but shimmers with realism nonetheless: one more example of Debussy's ability to transform artifice almost magically into a musical portrait of the real thing.

Yet the peace and seclusion that Debussy so ardently desired in which he might perform his magical experiments in music was shattered once more by controversy in 1907. Formerly, Debussy's followers had only had to pit themselves against the school of Franck, but now he was compared unfavourably with d'Indy, director of the influential *Schola Cantorum* and an aristocrat whose refined technique was seen as preferable to Debussy's. Similarly, Ravel, with whom Debussy had maintained guarded mutual admiration despite earlier quarrels, was now set up as Debussy's superior. Debussy responded by writing to a friend concerning

Poissons d'or: Chinese lacquerwork

Ravel's rather arch use of musical humour in his recently performed song cycle *Histoires naturelles*:

Do you honestly believe there is such a thing as musical humour? If two chords put their feet up in the air or adopt any other strange position they will never be humorous in themselves and could only become amusing by being empirical. It's true that Ravel is greatly talented, but I'm annoyed by his conjurer's attitude, or one might call it that of a fakir who casts spells and makes flowers break out of chairs. Unfortunately, conjuring tricks have to be prepared and when you've seen them the first time, you're not astonished anymore.

Paul Dukas

Neither Debussy nor Ravel wished to be rivals – Ravel admired and was influenced greatly by Debussy and was one of the *claque* who shouted most vociferously in support of *Pelléas et Mélisande* during its stormy first performances – but the public thrived on opposition, relishing each critical attack as it appeared, so it is not surprising that Ravel is supposed to have said of his inevitable estrangement from Debussy: 'It is probably best that we be on frigid terms for purely illogical reasons.'

The same thing happened with Paul Dukas, one of the few friends that Debussy had kept after his divorce from Lily. This composer, who was so fastidious that he only allowed fifteen of his works to be published and whose name is kept alive almost exclusively by his symphonic scherzo *The Sorcerer's Apprentice*, had written an opera based on another Maeterlinck text *Ariane et Barbe-bleu* which also had a Mélisande as one of Bluebeard's wives. It was performed at the *Opéra-Comique* in 1907, alternating with *Pelléas et Mélisande*, which Debussy had introduced successfully to Brussels in January. Immediately, those who considered Debussy's 'Impressionism' dangerous and vague held up this other Maeterlinck opera, with its rigidly observed use of classical forms, as a vastly superior antidote, and attached it to the d'Indy faction, much to the annoyance of both Debussy and Dukas.

The merits of both these operas could be compared at that time in the comfort of wealthy homes without having to endure the clamour of the opera house. In order to popularise its services, the Parisian telephone system offered the 'Théâtrephone' on which its subscribers could listen to an entire performance relayed from the opera house. It was in these circumstances that the reclusive Marcel Proust listened to *Pelléas et Mélisande* without having to leave his cork-lined room and come into contact with the public who were so injurious to his sensibilities. But Debussy, although wishing for the same seclusion, could not cut himself off from controversy by slamming down the telephone – he was in the thick of it. Maggie Teyte, who was to become the second legendary

Mélisande, met Debussy at this time for private coaching in the role and left a reminiscence of the mysterious composer simmering with rage under a frosty exterior:

Mary Garden had created and made a great success as Mélisande in the first performance of Debussy's opera. Then she had gone to America, and the wife of the director of the opera 'Comique' who disliked this young rival – to put it mildly – was determined she should not sing the part again. I also was out of favour. But when it was rumoured that Mary was returning from America I found myself thrust into the part of Mélisande to stop Miss Garden singing it. So it was, that at the age of eighteen, very small and light, I found myself on Debussy's doorstep, with the score of 'Pelléas' under my arm.

He was living then in a house off the Avenue du Bois which backed onto the Ceinture, the railway that runs all round Paris. It must have been a noisy situation for a composer and indeed one of Debussy's critics said 'Oh, now I understand why his music is such a beastly noise.' . . . He seemed tall but thick and heavy and he slouched rather than walked. He had a black beard and a square head covered with black hair. It struck me he had an almost Oriental look . . . All this I took in as he sat at the piano without even moving. There seemed to be hours of silence. At last he turned round: 'Vous êtes Mlle Teyte?' 'Oui Monsieur.' Silence. 'Vous êtes Mlle Maggie Teyte?' 'Oui Monsieur.' Silence. 'Mais, êtes-vous Mlle Maggie Teyte de l'Opéra-Comique?' 'Oui Monsieur.' He didn't believe it. 'Une autre anglaise – Mon Dieu.' Mary Garden had been the first Mélisande, a Scotswoman – now another – because we were both Scotswomen. Ah well. And so Mlle Teyte – anglaise, really écossaise, became an instrument in his hand. Strange to relate he never shook hands with me. He said to me, 'I will have Mélisande as I want her.' I was only too ready to agree.

As a teacher he was pedantic – that's the only word. Really pedantic. I'll give you an instance to show what I mean. He sat one day at the piano. He never played without getting into the mood. This took two or three minutes. I sat and waited. He raised his arms and was just ready to play when he saw a little bit of white cotton on the floor. He stopped and picked it up. He rolled it up and looked everywhere for a place to put it. Dead silence for another five minutes . . .

It is not easy to describe the impact of Debussy's character on me. He was such a many-sided character . . . He was volcanic: a volcano that smouldered. I once saw him so white with anger, then red with the sheer effort of control. There was a core of anger and bitterness in him – I often think he was rather like Golaud in 'Pelléas' and yet he wasn't. He was – it's all in his music – a very sensual man. No one seemed to like him. Jean Perrier, who played Pelléas to my Mélisande, went white with anger if you mentioned the name of Debussy . . .

Altogether my impression of him was of a man obsessed. But he showed another and more pleasant side of his nature when he was with his daughter Chou-Chou . . .

This portrait of Debussy, veering between anger and

Maggie Teyte as Mélisande

aristocratic aloofness, is undoubtedly accurate of the man at this time, his natural temperament exacerbated by the continual petty squabbles that surrounded his work. Like a swarm of gnats it continued to buzz about his ears so infuriatingly that he felt himself estranged from even those contemporaries he admired, especially d'Indy and his influential *Schola Cantorum* which was to spawn many important French composers in the early part of the twentieth century. Yet one consolation was the increasing interest his music was arousing in England – a country he had often admired. After a performance of his *String Quartet* in London and three important northern cities, Debussy was invited to conduct his *Prélude à l'après-midi d'un faune* and *La Mer* at the Queen's Hall in London – home of Sir Henry Wood's first Promenade Concerts – on 1 February 1908. There it received its first appreciative response from audiences that only a year before had applauded *Pelléas et Mélisande* enthusiastically at Covent Garden. At last Debussy found himself fêted in the drawing-rooms of London and reviewed sympathetically in the press by a public that had forgotten the death of its own Aesthetic Movement and the consequent scorn poured on all its French influences.

Other performances of *Pelléas et Mélisande* that year, with Mary Garden, in Berlin, Munich and La Scala Milan, brought further recognition, though less favourably in Germany and Italy than in America, where the response was so gratifying at the Manhattan Opera House in Oscar Hammerstein's production that the director of the rival Metropolitan, Giulio Gatti-Casazza, went to visit Debussy in Paris during May to buy the rights to those other operas that Debussy was rumoured to be writing. Gatti-Casazza later gave an account of this to the *New York Times*:

When I asked him to grant me the production rights for the Metropolitan for his three operas, the titles of which had already appeared in the newspapers – i.e. *La Légende de Tristan, La Chute de la maison Usher*, and *Le Diable dans le beffroi*, Debussy said: 'I must tell you honestly that of the three works, there barely exists the sketches of the librettos; and as to the music, I have written only some vague ideas. How can I honestly sell you such embryonic compositions?' 'Never mind,' I answered. 'The Metropolitan is happy to obtain the rights for what you can do and I beg you to sign an agreement with me.'

It was only through great efforts that I succeeded in obtaining the signature of Debussy and made him accept an advance of money which he himself wanted to be very modest. I recall that when I was leaving him he said: 'Do not forget that I am a lazy composer and that I sometimes require weeks to decide upon one harmonious accord in preference to another. Remember also that you are the one who insisted on making this agreement and that probably you will not receive anything.'

Alas! Poor Debussy was in this instance a prophet. Every year, when I was going to Paris, I would not fail to pay him a visit, as we had for each other much sympathy and friendship. And each time he would say to me: 'I am so happy to see you again, the more so because you do not ask me if I have finished one of my three operas. I must tell you that what increases in me is not geniality but uncertainty and laziness.'

Another contact with America was made through the violinist Arthur Hartmann with whom he struck up a friendship in 1908. Debussy even thought of visiting America with the American violinist, but this came to nothing. However, Hartmann was one of the few who penetrated the seclusion of Debussy's home and he later described these visits. Debussy would meet him in his study where Chinese vases, ornamental cats, wood carvings, tapestries and various musical instruments formed the chief décor. There was no evidence of any manuscripts and the only work area appeared to be a long bare table and a prim upright piano with no sheet music on it. The composer himself chain-smoked and rarely spoke. If there was an item of interest in a newspaper he would silently point it out to his visitor, but say nothing. If he had something important to communicate he would speak in hesitant monosyllables and detached utterances, his eyes half-closed all the while. The only real emotion he showed, as Maggie Teyte had noticed, was for his daughter. On one occasion, Hartmann recalls, they were playing with her in the garden when the doorbell rang. As though feeling that his little enclosed world had been threatened, Debussy made them all hide behind a bush until the unwelcome visitor had gone away.

It was to Chou-Chou, who was learning the piano at this time, that Debussy dedicated his *Children's Corner Suite* 'with her father's affectionate apologies for what follows'. When it was first performed by the pianist Harold Bauer at a *Cercle Musical* concert in December 1908 it was greatly applauded, despite Debussy's fear that its humour would not be appreciated. Some of the pieces were inspired by the toy animals in Chou-Chou's nursery and were given quaint titles in Debussy's defective English as a tribute to England, the continued vogue of Englishness in Paris at the time, and Chou-Chou's English governess. As a further tribute to England, the guards' military march he had heard three years earlier in London is jauntily up-tempoed to a *Golliwogg's Cakewalk* (sic) – a popular dance based on the new craze for ragtime jazz from America which was popular in Paris just then.

A more serious work written that year was his only *a cappella* music – the *Trois Chansons de Charles d'Orléans* – in which Debussy, eclectic as always, paid tribute to the great polyphonists he had admired in the little church in Rome during his student days. Despite their archaic form they were reasonably well received, although not unanimously.

Earlier in the year the controversy surrounding Debussy, his

Title page of the *Children's Corner Suite*, 1908

followers and opponents, led one newspaper to ask the composer if he was really the leader of a new school. His reply: 'There are no longer any schools of music: the chief task of musicians nowadays is to avoid outside influences' is typical of a composer who was so individual that he composed little, for fear of repeating his own recognised style. It was misunderstood, however, and the interviewer, one Maurice Leclerq, like all journalists with a nose for a story, canvassed many leading musicians of the time asking them the same question. The views he then published were generally superficial and irrelevant but were to cause the composer some distress when gathered together and published in book form at a later date.

Nothing could have been further from Debussy's real considerations than whether or not he led a new school of music. He had been feeling tired and ill and had begun to imagine that he was suffering from 'that fashionable disease Neurasthenia', as he said in one letter. He also felt drawn towards outsiders at this time signing himself 'Hamlet' in another letter, 'that elegant neurasthenic', as he called him, and lived much in the imaginary world of the House of Usher, taking up the opera again after the Metropolitan's commission. He wrote to Durand in the summer:

These days I have been working hard on *The Fall of the House of Usher* . . . There are moments when I lose the feeling of things around me and if the sister of Roderick Usher were to come into my house, I shouldn't be very surprised.

And again:

I am guilty of about ten acts of incivility an hour.

The opera was to chart, as Debussy said, 'the progress of anguish', although some of his own financial anguish was no doubt relieved by the arrival of two thousand francs from the Metropolitan that October for this and the other Poe opera, *The Devil in the Belfry*.

Debussy was persuaded to come out of his seclusion to revisit London at the beginning of 1909 to conduct his *Nocturnes* at the Queen's Hall once more. He accepted, for at least he knew he had a discriminating following there without nit-picking journalists attempting to drum up copy. Yet, shortly before he set off, his health broke. He was in so much pain that he had to consult a specialist who diagnosed, not fashionable Neurasthenia but, cancer of the stomach.

9 Travel and Seclusion

The shock of learning of his dreadful and incurable disease did not prevent Debussy from appearing twice in London early in 1909. Although taking morphine for the pain, he conducted his *Prélude à l'après-midi d'un faune* and *Nocturnes* to such appreciative applause that, as he wrote to his publisher: '*Fêtes* was encored and it only depended on me to get an encore for *L'après-midi d'un faune*. But I was ready to drop – a very bad posture for conducting anything.'

Financial considerations had forced him to undergo this ordeal, for his legal battles with his wife's ex-husband over alimony had put his lifestyle on the Bois de Boulogne in jeopardy, but there was great goodwill towards the French in England at that time. The English King-Emperor, Edward VII, had just visited Paris and signed the *Entente Cordiale* – a loose alliance between Britain and France designed to exclude the scheming German Kaiser Wilhelm II from expanding militarily and colonially – and Debussy felt that, although his own visit to London enhanced his personal prestige, he was being exploited in a political sense. Writing of that same triumphal concert in London he said:

I have to go to a reception organised by the Musicians' Club. What sort of a figure will I cut? I shall look like a man condemned to death. I can't get out of it, apparently because of the *Entente Cordiale* and other sentimental conceptions, most likely calculated to hasten the death of others.

Whether Debussy was being prophetic or just cynical in his allusion to these diplomatic manoeuvres as hastening the death of others is uncertain, but what is certain is that he would eventually see his gloomy prediction realised.

Debussy's second appearance in London in May that year found him much weaker. *Pelléas et Mélisande* was being performed at Covent Garden and he was there to advise on the production. But on the night of its triumph he was prostrate in his hotel room. Writing of that night he said:

They demanded the composer for a quarter of an hour, but he was peacefully reposing at his hotel suspecting no such glory. The conductor . . . Campanini was twice recalled and telephoned me that the opera was an enormous success, such as has rarely been known in England. He came to see me the next morning to tell me about it in his Punchinello manner and embraced me as if I were some medal blessed by the Pope.

Critics were unanimous in their praise, one noting that only Richard Strauss and Wagner had had as much success in London in recent years.

Although controversy still raged around him, Debussy was offered and accepted an official post in the National School of Music in Paris early that year. His task was basically to judge competitions and it was in that capacity that later in the year he wrote a Rhapsody for clarinet and piano as a test piece with more pleasure than he had tackled that other occasional piece for saxophone for Mrs Hall. This was later orchestrated by his own hand. That year also the various replies that Maurice Leclerq had received for his questionnaire on Debussy were published as a book under the title *Le Cas Debussy*. Amongst the absurdities it printed were the usual statements that Debussy's music made the listener ill, that it was unoriginal and morbid, that the composer was suffering from a nervous affliction he was conveying to others and that *Pelléas et Mélisande* would soon be forgotten, although one or two gleams of appreciation lightened this prevailing darkness.

The Fall of the House of Usher: illustration to Baudelaire's translation by Martin van Maöle

The real illness that Debussy was suffering from was now partly controlled by drugs, but there may have been some substance to the claim that he was also suffering from a nervous affliction at this time. Still working on *The Fall of the House of Usher* in seclusion he seemed to identify himself with the character of Roderick, so hypersensitive that he could feel the walls in his house suffering and whose condition Poe described as 'a nervous agitation . . . acute bodily illness of a mental disorder . . . a mind from which darkness poured forth upon all objects of the moral and physical universe in one unceasing radiation of gloom'. Writing again to Durand later in the year Debussy said:

I have almost finished a long monologue of poor Roderick. It almost makes the stones weep . . . as a matter of fact it is all about the influence of stones on the minds of neurasthenic people. The mustiness is charmingly rendered by contrasting the low notes of the oboe with harmonics of the violin (a patent device of my own). Don't speak of this to anyone; I think a great deal of it.

And again: 'I have got into the way of thinking about nothing else but Roderick Usher and *The Devil in the Belfry*', whilst a year later, still immersed in Poe's 'mansion of gloom' he said: 'I spend my existence in the House of Usher . . . and leave with my nerves as taut as the strings of a violin.'

Yet it would seem that such fits of composition were only confined to certain needs, for he also finished his sunny three movement score *Ibéria* as a tribute to the Spain he admired from afar and which he had only visited on a day trip across the frontier some years before. He also completed his *Rondes de printemps* based on a French folk song, an 'elusive' work as he called it, the two works being combined in his orchestral *Images* in that year. Only the third piece, *Gigues*, a tribute to England based on the Northumbrian *Keel Row* continued to give him trouble. Originally planned for two pianos, the *Images* represented a new departure for Debussy. He had written at first that he was trying:

to achieve something different – an effect of reality . . . what some idiots term Impressionism, a word that is altogether misused, particularly by the critics, since they do not hesitate to apply it to Turner, the finest creator of mysterious effects in all the world of art.

Serge Diaghilev

The year 1909 saw the first visit of the *Ballets Russes* to Paris, appearing at the *Châtelet*. This, the unofficial Russian ballet under the direction of the colourful impresario Serge Diaghilev included such brilliant talents as the set designer Leon Bakst, the choreographer Mikhail Fokin and the now legendary principal male dancer Vaslav Nijinksy. After the classical tutus of French ballet they burst on the jaded Paris scene like a multi-coloured bomb, including in their first season the *Polovtsian Dances* from Borodin's opera *Prince Igor*.

Debussy, whose interest in, and respect for, Russian music had always been profound, left the House of Usher to see this brilliant phenomenon and, like the entire ballet-loving population was overwhelmed by the colourful sets and costumes as well as the energetic music and dancing.

In February 1910, *Ibéria* was performed for the first time at the *Concerts Colonne*. It was applauded loudly and an encore was demanded, but many critics thought it pseudo-Spanish and compared it unfavourably with Albéniz's recently-published set of piano pieces also called *Iberia*. Debussy was known to have admired these, praising the impression they gave of 'flower-scented Spanish evenings' but his own work seemed to rise to the same level. Other critics cited examples by French and even Russian composers which they thought superior: Chabrier's *España*, Ravel's *Rapsodie espagnole* and Rimsky-Korsakov's *Caprice espagnole* being the most famous; but *Le Matin* carried a perceptive critique by Alfred Bruneau:

These delicate Spanish sketches bear no resemblance to the bold canvases of Albéniz and Chabrier . . . They contain no trace of violence or roughness, in spite of the lively gaiety that animates the first and last sections. They are delightfully poetical, exquisite in colouring, full of fascinating charm and marvellous artistry.

One young Spanish composer who had come to live in Paris in 1907 wrote of:

The echoes from the village . . . which seem to float in a clear atmosphere of scintillating light; the intoxicating spell of Andalusian nights; the festive gaiety of a people dancing . . . all this whirls in the air, approaches and recedes and our imagination is continually kept awake and dazzled by the power of an intensely expressive and richly varied music.

This was Manuel de Falla – eventually to become the leading Spanish composer of his age – who at this time was so impressed by Debussy's portrait of his homeland that he began writing his own *Nights in the Gardens of Spain* in which the influences of Debussy's score are obvious.

A few days after *Ibéria* had had its première, the other completed portion of *Images: Rondes de printemps*, was performed at the rival *Concerts Durand* with Debussy conducting. 'This is musical impressionism of a very special kind and very rare quality', the programme note announced, but the audience was not as enthusiastic and most critics saw the work as slight. However, Debussy found a champion in Ravel who wrote of the:

vivid charm and exquisite freshness of the *Rondes de printemps* and of those who 'were moved to tears by that dazzling *Ibéria* and its intensely disturbing 'Parfums de la Nuit' . . . So too was I, and so were Messrs Igor Stravinsky, Florent Schmitt, Roger Ducasse, Albert Roussel and a host of young composers whose productions are not unworthy of notice.

Debussy had already written to his publisher Durand concerning *Rondes de printemps:*

I am getting to believe more and more that music in its essence is not a thing that can be poured into a rigorous and traditional mould. It is made of colours and rhythmical beats. All the rest is a fraud, invented by cold-blooded imbeciles riding on the backs of the masters.

But all these pronouncements were meant for a musical élite. The Press was more interested in certain of Debussy's long-cherished projects, the *Courrier Musical* demanding querulously on 1 May: 'What Is M. Debussy Doing?', and informing its readership that he

is finishing two works by Edgar Poe . . . He is also finishing a *Tristan* to words by M. Gabriel Mourey based on an adaptation by M. Bedier, and he intends to write an *Orphée* to words by Max Anély [the pen-name of Victor Segalen] at present interpretation officer in Peking. This work will introduce parts sung without orchestral accompaniment which will surely be a novelty.

Yet the public saw nothing of these works that year, the only compositions to appear being two sets of songs – *Le Promenoir de deux amants* – in which he chose the troubadour-style poems of Tristan Lhermite and indulged archaic effects that might have originally been intended for the unrealised 'troubadour' opera *Tristan et Yseult* alluded to in the article above, and the *Trois Ballades* of the Medieval poet François Villon where he continued to delve into the traditions of France but with a more angular and abrasive style.

In June 1910 the *Ballets Russes*, following up the success of the previous year, returned to Paris with two sparkling new ballets. *Scheherazade*, based on Rimsky-Korsakov's dramatic orchestral suite, and an entirely new work commissioned from the young Stravinsky, *The Firebird*, were performed at the *Opéra*. Debussy saw them both. He was with a group of friends that included the controversial critic 'Willy' and his wife, the novelist Colette, when he attended the performance of *Scheherazade*. With Bakst's opulent costumes and sets, Nijinsky and the exotic Jewess Ida Rubinstein in the cast, the occasion was a sensation which Paris had never witnessed before. It was to initiate a new craze in decorative art and oriental 'Russianness'. Whole salons were to be transformed overnight into imitations of Bakst's barbaric splendours and women draped themselves in flowing gowns modelled on his costumes. Debussy did not go that far – his taste remained one of Chinese refinement – but, according to Colette, after seeing *Scheherazade*, they all went to a mutual friend's house where Debussy:

Claude Debussy at the Châtelet

was exultant. He sang scraps of this new music, accompanied himself with a glissando on the piano, imitated the timpani on a pane of glass, the glockenspiel on a crystal vase. He hummed like a swarm; he laughed with his whole astonishing visage – and we were delighted.

This glimpse of Debussy in one of his rare extrovert moods contrasts strongly with the solemn and withdrawn appearance he usually presented to the world and testifies profoundly to the effect Diaghilev's company had on him. Debussy was also enthusiastic about Stravinsky's first major score, possibly because it betrayed the fingerprints of his teacher Rimsky-Korsakov. He described the young Russian, who had recently come to stay in

Paris, as 'the most wonderful orchestral craftsman of the age' and a mutual respect grew up between the two composers which was eventually to become a guarded friendship.

The Metropolitan Opera of New York also appeared in Paris that season at the *Châtelet*. Caruso and Toscanini headed an impressive cast in a repertoire which included Verdi's operas *Aida* and *Falstaff*. Debussy sat in Gatti-Casazza's box throughout these performances, impressed, especially by *Falstaff* which he could hardly believe Verdi had written when he was almost eighty. Debussy and Toscanini had an emotional meeting afterwards for both admired each other deeply and Debussy was especially grateful to Toscanini for introducing *Pelléas et Mélisande* so sensitively to the Italians, weathering all manner of abuse for his pains, including a riot at La Scala in 1908.

Gatti-Casazza also accompanied Debussy to the *Ballets Russes* and left an account of Debussy's latest interest and the fate of the operas so tantalisingly offered to the public earlier in the year:

'You know,' he told me, 'the operas that I am to write for you will be further delayed on account of a new fact.'

'But what fact?' I asked.

'I will not write an opera, but a ballet, because, after all, it is better to have to do with mimes than with singers.'

'Well,' I said, 'let us make an agreement also for a ballet.'

'Oh no,' interrupted Debussy. 'Never! I have already abused enough of your courtesy, faith and patience. No contract; and when the ballet is finished I shall offer it to the Metropolitan before anyone else.'

I recall that after the performance I accompanied Debussy to his house in the Avenue du Bois. He spoke to me at length about *Le Diable dans le beffroi* and *La Chute de la maison Usher*, the libretti of which, as is known, had been taken from the tales of Edgar Poe.

'But you know,' he continued, 'Edgar Poe possessed the most original fantasy among the literature of all lands; he found a note absolutely new and different.'

To this I replied: 'It is true, and that is the precise reason why such a poet's ideas need to be clothed with the music of a unique composer like yourself, maestro.'

'Perhaps my dear Gatti,' he rejoined, 'this investiture will never be heard by anyone. I fear as much. I am getting older and more lazy than ever. Good night and adieu!' . . .

I never saw Claude Debussy again, and, alas! I never saw a note of the operas of which the Metropolitan had been so proud to procure the rights.

But Debussy was not writing a ballet. With the example of his beloved Chopin before him he was composing a set of twelve preludes for piano. Nearly all of these had some literary or extra-musical title alluding, not only to Poe's 'City in the Sea' and the legends of the sunken cathedral of Ys – a subject that had also occupied Debussy's contemporary Lalo in his opera *Le Roi d'Ys* – but Baudelaire, harlequins and seaside minstrels such as he would have seen on his holidays at fashionable Cabourg, bells, antique dancers and the wind. This set also included one of his most famous pieces: *The Girl with the Flaxen Hair*. Debussy wrote the title of each piece at the end of the score, however, so that it would be judged first and foremost as music although the virtuosity and wide-ranging imagination of these works does at times hide an occasionally pedestrian reshaping of old material, as some critics remarked when both Debussy and Ricardo Viñes introduced selected numbers that year.

In December, Debussy was invited to conduct various concerts throughout the then ailing Austro-Hungarian empire, and accepted mainly for his pressing need for concert receipts although, as he told his publisher at the time: 'One would need the heroism of a commercial traveller, and one must be willing to compromise, and that is most repugnant to me.' He chose to introduce *Ibéria* in Vienna, with the tried favourite *Prélude à l'après-midi d'un faune* and a version of the early *Petite Suite* orchestrated by Debussy's friend and colleague Henri Büsser. He found that he had to rehearse with the aid of an interpreter which proved to be a frustrating experience for one suffering from a painful disease. Afterwards he wrote to Durand:

It was no joke . . . and my nerves are shattered . . . Well, they managed to understand in the end, and I got what I wanted out of them. I was

The Theater an der Wien, Vienna

recalled as often as a dancer; the only reason why the idolizing crowd did not unyoke the horses from my carriage was that I was in a taxi-cab.

Interviewed afterwards, Debussy was asked once more about his 'school'. Rattled, he replied: 'There is no school of Debussy. I have no disciples. I am I.' Of the great intellectual ferment then going on in the chief capital of this ramshackle empire Debussy cared hardly at all – Mahler, Schoenberg and the Expressionist art of Klimt and Kokoschka; the psychology of Freud; the new movements in architecture and philosophy – all were masked by a cloud of illness and bad temper at being pestered so publicly by admirers.

He next moved on to Budapest, the twin capital, where fifteen hundred people attended a chamber concert that included Debussy's *String Quartet* and *Children's Corner Suite*. Debussy was faintly embarrassed by this huge response to such a small-scale concert, but the Hungarians treated him as a celebrity, publishing long articles about him in the Press. Despite this, Debussy was not very impressed by the Hungarian capital, then showing all the anachronism of the doomed Austrian political experiment, and he ironically remarked it was, 'an old city with too much "make-up" where you get a surfeit of Brahms and Puccini and where the officers have bosoms like women and the women bosoms like officers.'

Yet Budapest was musically more interesting than this wry comment would suggest, for it provided new experiences for a composer always interested in ethnic music and novel effects. He heard the Tzigane – that quintessentially Hungarian dance – played on the violin so authentically by the great exponent Radics that he wrote: 'In an ordinary commonplace café he gave me the impression of being seated in the shade of a great forest. He draws from the soul a special brand of melancholy.' Debussy also heard the cimbalom, then an instrument almost exclusively played in cafés and bars, and was so inspired by it that he wrote a short-waltz of his own – *La Plus que lente* – which neatly summed up his experiences of Vienna and Budapest by including a cimbalom in the orchestration.

On his return to Vienna a banquet was held with Debussy as guest of honour. At this, an official made a speech in which he tried to compliment the composer by suggesting his musical experiments had 'abolished melody'. Debussy, in his reply, acidly replied: 'But, my dear sir, my music aims at nothing but melody.'

Returning finally to Paris, exhausted, Debussy sat down to consider a letter he had received in November. It seemed at last the invitation he had been waiting for: to escape petty vexations in a noble and mystical project that would engage all his genius.

10 Return to the Theatre

Gabriele d'Annunzio

The Italian poet Gabriele d'Annunzio, a colourful and volatile figure, was seeking Debussy's collaboration. Although only a year younger than the composer, he was much more a man of the world, involving himself in Italian politics and the theatre for which he wrote densely Symbolist plays. He had long admired Debussy's music and, inspired by an infatuation for Ida Rubinstein, had written a 'Mystery' in five 'mansions' (Acts) on the theme of the Martyrdom of St Sebastian. In asking Debussy to write the music he said:

I have dreamed for a long time of the bleeding youth transfigured in the Christian myth, like the beautiful wounded god mourned by the women of Byblus before the catafalque of ebony and purple in the Vernal Equinox. I had chosen this line from a verse of Veronica Gambara, the great Italian poetess of the Renaissance: 'He that loved me most, wounds me.' My mystery play is a development of this theme.

The figure of Sebastian had exercised a fascination on the creative minds of the *décadence* for some years. He was seen as an image of the suffering artist, and d'Annunzio's obsession was certainly not unique. His was a precious and stylised play, written in stilted French, but it appealed to Debussy's love of the exquisite and his feelings that religion was basically an aesthetic experience. He too shared the vision of Christ united with the figure of Adonis in the beautiful but androgynous Sebastian, Archer of God at the court of the pagan Emperor Diocletian and, leaving the morbidities of Poe, set about writing the music with an energy and fervour he seemed unable to bring to his long-cherished operatic projects.

The play was scheduled for performance in May 1911 at the *Châtelet*, so Debussy engaged André Caplet who had just finished orchestrating Debussy's *Gigues* and *Children's Corner Suite* to help him orchestrate this new score. He locked the doors of his house to visitors and retired into seclusion, admitting only a few friends but, curiously, several journalists who were eager to interview him on his latest project. One, Henri Malherbe, received the most revealing insights which he published in *The Excelsior* that February:

M. Claude Debussy, in his quest for light and silence, has withdrawn to a bright, secluded little corner, not far from the Bois de Boulogne. In his narrow study which is most artistically decorated in fabrics of bronze and tawny hues, a deliberate simplicity reigns. The only objects that reveal the musician are a long Japanese kito and the bulky form of a small, black piano. The composer of *Pelléas* has the dusky, golden countenance of an idol. His aspect is at once powerful, noble and unusual. His short beard and black hair help the illusion; he looks like one of the Magi who has strayed by mistake into our times . . . He is slow to give his confidence. He has withdrawn within his mortal shell, into the domain of pure feeling . . . In these elegant surroundings, M. Debussy rolls a cigarette like any artisan, and speaks in a voice at first high-pitched and drawling which, as it increases in tone, becomes deep and pleasant . . .

The almost hieratic image of a prophet which the journalist evokes underlines the views that Debussy then expounded on religion, which almost amounted to a musician's quasi-pagan creed:

I do not practise religion in accordance with the sacred rites. I have made mysterious Nature my religion. I do not believe that a man is any closer to God for being clad in priestly garments, nor that one place in a town is better adapted to meditation than another . . . Nature in all its vastness is truthfully reflected in my sincere though feeble soul . . . and my hands unconsciously assume an attitude of adoration . . . To feel the supreme and moving beauty of the spectacle to which Nature invites her ephemeral guests! – that is what I call prayer . . . Who will discover the secret of musical composition? The sound of the sea, the curve of the horizon, the wind in the leaves, the cry of a bird register complex impressions within us. Then suddenly without any deliberate consent on our part, one of these memories issues forth to express itself in the language of music . . . I detest doctrines and their impertinent implications. And for that reason I wish to write down my musical dreams in a spirit of utter self-detachment. I wish to sing of my interior visions with the naive candour of a child. No doubt this simple musical grammar will jar on some people. It is bound to offend the partisans of deceit and artifice. I forsee that and I rejoice at it. I shall do nothing to create adversaries, but neither shall I do anything to turn enmities into friendships. I must endeavour to be a great artist, so that I may dare to be myself and suffer for my faith. Those who feel as I do will only appreciate me more. The others will shun and hate me.

In these last words, especially, it would seem that Debussy had identified himself with Sebastian as an image of the suffering faith of the artist, as Oscar Wilde had also done after his disgrace. As with Hamlet and Roderick Usher, the identification has something of the fashionable pose of the artist as a target for the ignorance of the masses, but Debussy's ideas and his own physical suffering at this time transcend such considerations for his illness had made his work doubly difficult. When he sent the music to Durand in April he wrote:

I admit that I'm not displeased with it. But, as I've told you several times, I'm at the end of my tether.

Rehearsals began immediately. The sets and costumes were designed by Bakst, but in an inappropriate oriental style that seemed to hark back to his *Scheherazade* designs for Diaghilev, and Ida Rubinstein's performance would be most charitably described as bizarre. Yet Debussy had said that he was 'so happy and proud . . . to illustrate M. d'Annunzio's work in music' and wept both when he played the music through to Durand on the piano and at these first rehearsals. Despite other problems of presenting a work requiring choruses on stage, members of that chorus were also reduced to tears by the music according to one account. At times sensual, at others dramatic, grief-stricken and eerie in a style that must have had something to do with the House of Usher, the music made a deep impression on many involved in its performance.

But there were to be further problems. This 'mystery' with music by a confessed pagan, a Jewish dancer impersonating a Christian saint and the identification of that saint with Adonis raised many orthodox religious hackles. The Archbishop of Paris put the play on the Index forbidding Catholics to see it and hinting at excommunication for any who did, then a Press campaign led by fervent Catholic journalists echoed his sentiments.

Despite the laws passed during President Grévy's administration in the latter part of the nineteenth century establishing France as a secular state, and further laws passed in 1905 finally separating Church and State, the influence of the Catholic church over the minds of Parisians was still considerable. As as result, subscribers withdrew their support and cancellations of tickets threatened to leave the *Châtelet* virtually empty for the Gala Performance. The author and the composer felt it necessary in these circumstances to publish a defence of their work:

The Archbishop of Paris, in a manner that was ill-advised, has attacked in his recent decree a work, still unknown to him, created by two artists who, in the course of several years of labour, have given at least evidence of their unremitting aspiration toward the severest form of art. Without

failing in the respect which the Archbishop's note itself fails to accord us, we desire to express our regret at the singular treatment which we have not deserved; and we affirm – upon our honour and upon the honour of all those who are acquainted with 'The Martyrdom of Saint Sebastian' – that this work, deeply religious, is the lyrical glorification, not only of the admirable athlete of Christ, but of all Christian heroism.

Debussy followed this up with an interview which was published in *Comoedia*:

Is it not obvious that a man who sees mystery in everything will be inevitably attracted to a religious subject? I do not wish to make a profession of faith. But, even if I am not a practising Catholic nor a believer, it did not cost me much effort to rise to the mystical heights which the poet's drama attains.

Let us be clear about the word *mysticism*. You see that this very day the Archbishop has forbidden the faithful to assist at d'Annunzio's play, although he does not know the work. But let us not dwell on these annoying details . . . From the artistic point of view such decrees cannot be considered, I assure you that I wrote my music as though I had been asked to do it for a church. The result is decorative music, if you like, a noble text interpreted in sounds and rhythms; and in the last act when the saint ascends into Heaven, I believe I have expressed all the feelings aroused in me by the thought of the Ascension. Have I succeeded? That no longer concerns me. We have not the simple faith of other days. Is the faith expressed by my music orthodox or not? I cannot say. It is my faith, my own, singing in all sincerity.

Sunday, 21 May, was marked for the first performance at which many notables were to be present, but that same morning an aeroplane went out of control at a race near Paris and killed the War Minister. The country went into official mourning so the managers of the *Châtelet* only admitted the Press to the performance which they renamed a rehearsal. Many people with tickets forced their way in nonetheless and Debussy seemed once more to be the cause of noisy disruption in the theatre in this, his first work for the stage since *Pelléas et Mélisande* had caused such a stir. The first official performance occurred the following day. It was barely adequate and, according to one report, the audience 'leaked away like water from a broken vase', but there were no ugly scenes and many of the critics wrote well of it, likening Debussy's music to *Parsifal*, although most realised that the play was destined to drag the music down into obscurity. Two performances of orchestral extracts were given at the *Société Musicale Indépendante* and the whole work was later performed in Boston and Italy, but in neither of these forms did it achieve any real success. It was not to be revived in Paris until 1922 when once more Ida Rubinstein, who controlled the rights, gave the

Ida Rubinstein in the role of St Sebastian: *Le Martyre de saint-Sébastien*, 1911. Watercolour by Leon Bakst

99

extraordinary performance that had helped damn the whole enterprise. In spite of Debussy later expressing an interest in transferring the work into an opera, he never succeeded in finding the right libretto, and the work has only maintained a limited hold on the fringes of the repertoire by being performed as an oratorio with selected extracts from the play spoken by a narrator.

After the relative failure of the work that had absorbed so much of his inspiration, Debussy was once more pressed with financial difficulties. As he often did on these occasions, he authorised the publication of some early works including the *Marche écossaise*, a piece originally commissioned and written for two pianos in 1899 but orchestrated later by the composer and performed for the first time in 1911. Such royalty-earners did nothing to increase Debussy's reputation amongst the critics. He also broke out of his seclusion and appeared in public performances of his works. He conducted Caplet's orchestration of the *Children's Corner Suite*, unheard in France before, and appeared as pianist in some of his new preludes. He also accompanied Maggie Teyte in the *Fêtes galantes* and *Le Promenoir des deux amants*. After the final performance of *Le Martyre de saint-Sébastien* he went to Turin to conduct a concert of French music. *L'après-midi d'un faune*, *Ibéria* and the *Children's Corner Suite* were included with works by Chabrier, Dukas and Roger Ducasse, and it was during his stay there that he met both Richard Strauss and Edward Elgar. His guarded admiration for Strauss is known, but his opinion of the English composer, then finishing his Second Symphony as a tribute to the recently deceased Edward VII, is unknown, although he could not have been drawn towards his teutonically-influenced classicism. Debussy was partly fascinated by the English and their exotic empire, and it may have been his meeting with Elgar that prompted an interest in the Coronation of George V and his imperial progress through India, where the Durbar of 1912 excited Debussy's curiosity sufficiently for him to write a prelude based on a newspaper report of the event the following year. Elgar, however, certainly did not understand Debussy's music and was later reported as having said that it 'lacked guts'.

On his return to Paris, Debussy received another commission for a stage work, once again for the personal glorification of a dancer. Maud Allen required a work that would provide an ecstatic and lengthy solo and *Khamma*, with a plot in which Debussy had a hand, is a series of three dances set in an ancient Egyptian temple where a girl dances herself to death before an idol. Debussy knew Florent Schmitt's *La Tragédie de Salomé* which had been premièred earlier in the year and which exploited much the same idea. He had also seen Stravinsky's *Petrouchka*, first performed at that season's appearance of the *Ballets Russes*,

Nijinsky in l'Après-midi d'un faune Leon Bakst

and the exoticism of these two remarkable scores seems to have fired him with enthusiasm for his own ballet, for he produced the piano score very quickly. It contains some brilliant and typical passages but, after the initial enthusiasm, Debussy felt unable to finish the orchestration and asked the composer Charles Koechlin to carry out this task under his direction. Once more, this proved a stumbling block and *Khamma*, although finally handed over to Maud Allen in 1916, was not produced during the composer's lifetime. Debussy later recalled the work with typical irony: 'that queer ballet with its trumpet calls suggesting a riot or an outbreak of fire', but this hardly does the work justice.

Perhaps feeling that he had done sufficient hackwork for one year, Debussy began writing and collecting together a second book of preludes for piano, yet the ballet continued to demand his attention. The *Ballets Russes* wanted to stage *Fêtes* and Debussy agreed that the principal dancer, Nijinsky, should also choreograph *L'après-midi d'un faune* and dance the name part in the 1912 season. So keen was Diaghilev to produce the ballet that the première of Ravel's full-length and opulent masterpiece *Daphnis et Chloë*, on which he had worked for three years, was delayed despite being scheduled to open the season. This caused more friction between the two composers, although much of this had to do with internal quarrels at the *Ballets Russes*. Nijinsky was an indifferent choreographer and although, as he stated in his diary, he 'loved creating it . . . Worked well, feeling the presence of God', the result was disappointing. Debussy wrote to Godet after seeing it:

Nijinsky's perverse genius is entirely devoted to peculiar mathematical processes. The man adds up demisemiquavers with his feet and proves the result with his arms. Then, as if suddenly stricken with partial paralysis, he stands listening to the music with a most baleful eye . . . It is ugly; Dalcrozian in fact.

Debussy's opinion was shared by both public and critics although Diaghilev bribed two unlikely reviewers to praise it: Odilon Redon the Symbolist painter complied, and the great sculptor Auguste Rodin wrote so glowing a report that Diaghilev helped to pay the rent on his studio at the Hôtel Biron for the rest of Rodin's life.

Despite the unpropitious partnership, Diaghilev persuaded the financially embarrassed Debussy to accept another commission for a ballet to be choreographed by Nijinsky. The result was *Jeux*, the 'games' of the title being both tennis and the underlying amorous games of three lovers. The synopsis gave a general idea of this:

The scene is a garden at dusk: a tennis ball has been lost; a young man and two girls are searching for it. The artificial light of the large electric lamps shedding fantastic rays about them suggests the idea of childish games: they play hide and seek, they try to catch one another, they quarrel, they sulk without cause. The night is warm; the sky is bathed in a pale light; they embrace. The spell is broken by another tennis ball thrown in mischievously by an unknown hand. Surprised and alarmed, the young man and the girls disappear into the nocturnal depths of the garden.

Despite this vague plot, Debussy knew what it really meant. He wrote to Stravinsky at the time: 'It expresses the "shocking" behaviour of three characters in an acceptable way', and Nijinsky wrote in his diary:

The story of this ballet is about three young men making love to each other . . . Debussy, the well-known composer, wanted the subject to be written down. I asked Diaghilev to help me to do this and with Bakst they wrote it down on paper . . . In the ballet, the two girls represent the two boys and the young man is Diaghilev. I changed the characters as love between three men could not be represented on the stage . . . Debussy did not like the subject . . . but he was paid 10,000 gold francs for this ballet and therefore had to finish it.

In spite of his misgivings, Debussy created a musical score that was both subtle and progressive, flirting at times with the twelve-tone process that Schoenberg's *Pierrot Lunaire*, which had just been performed in Berlin, also foreshadowed. Debussy's modernism however was of a more intensely private kind arrived at through his own experiments. He had no time for Schoenberg or other 'shocks'. This was the same year that the first part of Proust's long psychological novel *À la Recherche du Temps Perdu* was published in Paris. It was also the year when Marcel Duchamp exhibited his painting on glass, *Nude Descending a Staircase* – a series of contortions prefiguring 'Anti-Art' – and when someone cracked the glass by mistake the artist considered the work to be even finer. These experiments led nowhere in Debussy's opinion, but his score in some ways reflects the restlessness of the age in a ballet that Diaghilev and Nijinsky wanted to represent 'the spirit of Man in 1913'. Yet when this illustrious pair tried to see how the composer was getting on with the music by making an unannounced call in the summer of 1912, Debussy wrote: 'I refused to play them what I'd completed as I did not want barbarians nosing through my personal chemical experiments.'

Debussy took infinite pains over the score of *Jeux*, revising and re-orchestrating to the last moment. As he worked on it in the early part of 1913, other scores of his were receiving notice. *Gigues*, in Caplet's orchestration, was finally performed at the *Concerts Colonne* on 27 January. Debussy called the piece 'Sad gigues, tragic *gigues*' and the critics thought it a slight piece although Caplet defended it as representing the true nature of the composer. Shortly afterwards, a version of *Printemps* re-orchestrated by Henri Büsser drew muted applause and the usual cry of warmed-up fare and declining talent. In April, Debussy conducted *La Mer* and *Nuages* at a 'Festival of French Music' to open the new *Théâtre des Champs-Élysées* in company with d'Indy, Dukas and Fauré, whose opera *Pénélope* was produced there shortly afterwards, vying with the hundredth performance of *Pelléas et Mélisande* at the *Opéra-Comique*. In May, the egregious dancer Loïe Fuller performed *Nuages* and *Sirènes*. The Irish poet W.B. Yeats had seen her and wrote in one of his poems of her 'shining web, a floating ribbon of cloth'. Her use of Chinese silks

created a spectacle of shimmering enchantment that had little to do with her dancing or Debussy's music.

All this caused an atmosphere of expectation about Debussy's new ballet, but when it was produced on 15 May at the *Théâtre des Champs-Élysées* no one seemed to know what to make of it. The modern sets and costumes, so unlike the usual sumptuous *Ballets Russes* styles, and the angular dancing drew attention away from Debussy's subtle score so that there was only moderate approval. The critics were also divided. One mentioned its 'rich, expressive tone-colouring', another that its effects seemed 'more strained, more artificial', whilst another likened it to Dukas whose ballet *La Péri* had been performed at the rival *Châtelet* the month before.

Whether the public would have given *Jeux* a fairer hearing subsequently is uncertain for, two months later, the *Ballets Russes* staged Stravinsky's new *Rite of Spring*. This work burst onto the musical scene like a storm, its barbaric rhythms and percussive effects so scandalising its audiences that there were riots at every performance, completely upstaging Debussy's ballet. Debussy was not disheartened. Stravinsky visited him at his home the same month and, according to Louis Laloy, who was also present, they played the *Rite of Spring* together on the piano, Stravinsky sweating so profusely that he had to remove his collar. Afterwards, Debussy and Laloy were apparently so dumbfounded by this new music that they did not know what to say, but it would seem that, despite his personal liking for Stravinsky, Debussy did not entirely approve.

As relaxation from *Jeux*, Debussy took refuge in his family life. Pasteur Valéry-Radot who was a frequent visitor at this time remarked:

His wife surrounded him with affection, realising that, like a child, he had to be sheltered from the rough side of life. What gave him more genuine pleasure than anything else was to listen to his adorable little daughter Chou-Chou talking or singing, playing the piano, or dancing to some tune he had composed specially for her . . .

Claude Debussy and Igor Stravinsky

Jeux: Pastels by Valentine Hugo

Now he found inspiration from childhood through André Hellé who had adapted his children's book *La Boîte à joujoux* (The Box of Toys) into a ballet scenario and who asked Debussy to write the music. Debussy readily agreed. The story was like a slightly less sinister version of *Petrouchka* with the same love-crossed dolls and puppets, but with a happy ending. After seeing *Petrouchka*, Debussy had written to Stravinsky that he had composed with 'magic that mysteriously changes mechanical spirits into humans. So far I think you're the only one who has this magical ability'. Now Debussy, who was also fascinated by the quasi-humanity of puppets, dolls and clowns, wrote to Durand that he was:

105

Extracting confidences from a few of Chou-Chou's old dolls. A doll's soul is more mysterious than even Maeterlinck would credit and won't put up with the nonsense that pleases human souls.

Yet, although he managed to write the work in a few months, he could not face the task of orchestrating it and once more turned to the faithful André Caplet. He worked at this for another four years but, although it was not destined to be staged until after the composer's death, when it achieved a notable success, Debussy never lost interest in seeing the work performed. He discussed it occasionally with Hellé over the following years and maintained his affection for what he later described as: 'a pantomime to the kind of music I have written for children in Christmas and New Year albums . . . a little work to amuse the children, nothing more!'

In the same year, Debussy was finishing his second book of preludes with their revealing allusions to his more whimsical delights, including a music hall clown he had seen at the *Théâtre Marigny*; his Dickensian view of England, the Delhi Durbar and Peter Pan, as well as more impressionist set pieces evoking fogs, water, leaves, fireworks and a portrait of the Alhambra inspired by a postcard sent by Albéniz. He also returned to Mallarmé for the texts of *Trois Poèmes de Stéphane Mallarmé*. He was also indulging in occasional journalism and contributed reviews to the *Review S.I.M.* and the Paris edition of the *Journal of International Music* despite voicing a desire to hear as little new music as possible.

Then he embarked on the last in his round of international tours. He received an invitation from Serge Koussevitsky to revisit Russia to conduct some of his works in Moscow and St Petersburg that December, and went, despite arriving in the depths of a Russian winter. But the enthusiastic reception he received there did much to alleviate the chill. He met some of the younger composers who gave him a letter addressed to 'the illustrious master' when he passed through the twin cities that were soon to change so irrevocably, and he sought out his former pupil Sophie von Meck whom he had proposed to so many years before. He was then a successful middle-aged man suffering from cancer and she was a married woman involved with Women's Rights in a nation that had hardly any democratic institutions, yet although they had changed greatly, they must have enjoyed reminiscing about their youth.

In February 1914 he was in Rome where he was made a member of the Academy of St Cecilia where he conducted *La Mer*, *L'après-midi d'un faune* and *Rondes de printemps* to rapturous applause. Debussy was now revisiting the scenes of his quarrelsome youth in triumph, perhaps recalling visits with the von Mecks as much as his rather unhappy time at the Villa Medici.

He was next in Holland. The concerts he conducted at The Hague and Amsterdam brought him acclaim but, as he confessed, 'quite inconsiderable sums' of the money for which he always had such a pressing need. He conducted the *Nocturnes* and the *Prélude à l'après-midi d'un faune* as well as playing some of his new preludes, in concerts that contained works by other French composers.

He was now celebrated and most of the animosities he had aroused in others were forgotten. An attempt was now made to establish him by the academics he had despised for so long: the prestigious *Académie des Beaux Arts* offered him a place on its board but, although Debussy would have accepted, delays frustrated his election. Yet the adulation he received was little

Original edition of *La Boite à joujoux* by André Héllé

comfort to him. His illness continued to sap his energies whilst his travelling and constant public appearances only aggravated the condition. But he could not afford to ignore any offer of an engagement that might help him financially so he even accepted an offer to play at a private concert given at the home of Sir Edgar and Lady Speyer in London that June. The money he received for this was inadequate, he complained, but still 'a drop of water in the desert of these dreadful summer months'.

It was a particularly hot summer – that legendary final summer of Edwardian England and, for the student of international affairs, of Europe itself.

11 In Black and White

For more than a decade tensions had existed between the continental empires – Russia and France had formed alliances with each other, and France with the faintly isolated British empire, whilst Austria-Hungary and the pushy new German empire, led by its unstable military autocrat Wilhelm II, continued to press for more influence. On 28 June 1914 the seemingly insignificant assassination of the Austrian heir to the throne in the Serbian town of Sarajevo brought these tensions to a head. Exactly one month later Austria-Hungary declared war on Serbia, hoping for an easy conquest, but this declaration set off a whole domino-pack of alliances. Germany had armed itself for just such an opportunity: it found a pretext to declare war on its old enemy France on 3 August and on Belgium on 4 August. Entering Belgian territory with great savagery, massacring its people and burning, amongst other historic monuments, the great library of Louvain with its irreplaceable manuscripts, the German army pressed on towards France.

Events moved rapidly thereafter. Britain, honouring its alliances, declared war on Germany and British troops began to arrive in France to join the newly-mobilised French army. Debussy, back in Paris, was struck numb with the horror of it all. He watched the bizarre sight of troops leaving Paris for the Front in taxicabs. Other colleagues and composers, including Ravel, enlisted in the army, but Debussy, fifty-two years old and far too ill to join up, felt frustrated at his own uselessness. Remembering the Franco-Prussian war of his childhood, he wrote to Durand on 8 August:

You know I have *sang-froid* and certainly nothing of the army spirit. I've never had a rifle in my hands. My recollections of 1870 and the anxiety of my wife, whose son and son-in-law are in the army, prevent me from becoming very enthusiastic. All this makes my life intense and troubled. I am just a poor little atom crushed in this terrible cataclysm. What I am doing seems so wretchedly small. I've got to the state of envying Satie who, as a corporal, is really going to defend Paris. And so, my dear Jacques, if you have any work that you can give me do not forget me. Forgive me for counting on you, but you are really all I have.

And again:

My age and military qualifications would just about fit me to guard a fence – nothing more. But if another head is needed to ensure victory, I'll offer mine willingly . . .

Durand offered him work editing a new French edition of Chopin's Polonaises and Waltzes as part of a project to replace German editions of classical works, but as hostilities began on French soil, with Charleroi – just sixty miles from Paris – in flames, followed by defeats for the French and British troops at Mons and Le Câteau at the end of August, Debussy became so depressed that he could not work at all.

After this battle, the French Commander-in-Chief, Marshal Joffre, regrouped his army in and around Paris and launched a counter-offensive that drove the Germans back to the River Marne. Stalemate was reached with both lines digging in to oppose each other from trenches along a line from Verdun to the sea. By the end of the year three hundred and eighty thousand Frenchmen had been killed, but this was not to be the swift war that many had prophesied. Now began four years of the most savage mechanised slaughter ever witnessed during which one-tenth of French territory was continually occupied and one-and-a-quarter million Frenchmen were to die.

A garrison was brought in to defend Paris and on 22 September the Government left the capital for the relative safety of Bordeaux. As Debussy watched it all, he must have been reminded of the scenes of his childhood, culminating in the massacre of the Commune, and his anger against everything German rose higher. He wrote to Durand:

If I had the courage, or rather if I did not dread the inevitable blatancy natural to that type of composition, I should like to write a 'Marche Héroïque' . . . but I must say, I regard it as ridiculous to indulge in heroism, in all tranquility, well out of the reach of bullets.

When the English *Daily Telegraph* invited composers to contribute to 'King Albert's Album' in a tribute to the Belgian monarch 'and his soldiers', Debussy was inspired sufficiently to produce, not the blatantly military march he had feared, but a *Berceuse héroïque* for piano which he orchestrated in December. This 'heroic lullaby' is muted, with a melancholy reference to the Belgian national anthem, and is an appropriate reflection of the composer's grief at this time. Debussy wrote to Godet: 'This is all

I've been able to do. The fighting still going on so near has a physical effect on me, and, in addition, my ignorance of military matters worries me . . .' When this music was played the following year it was not understood. Something much more jingoistic had been expected.

Apart from this slight, but heart-felt, work Debussy composed nothing, but busied himself on the more routine editing of Chopin. He found it frustrating, feeling that he could not do sufficient justice to a composer he admired so greatly. He wrote to Durand:

I have a very clear recollection of what Mme Mauté de Fleurville told me. Chopin advised his pupils to study without the pedal and not to hold it except in very rare cases.

But later he wrote to Durand that the variants in the scores 'terrify me', although he eventually produced a workman-like edition.

Meanwhile his feeling for a national French music surfaced in a letter to his friend Valléry-Radot. Referring to the *Berceuse héroïque* he said:

I have begun again to write a little music, mostly so as not to forget it completely, very little for my own satisfaction . . . It seems to me there is an opportunity of reverting, not to a too narrow and contemporary French tradition, but to the real true one which one can place immediately after Rameau – just when it was beginning to be lost! . . . shall we have the courage? Shall we dare to extricate from the depths that have gradually been engulfing it, the true French clarity?

He expressed himself more forcefully in an article he wrote as a preface to *Pour la Musique Française*. Referring to Rameau and Couperin he said:

Where are our old clavecinists who had so much true music? They had the secret of gracefulness and emotion without epilepsy, which we have negated like ungrateful children . . . Today when all the virtues of our race are valiantly reasserting themselves, the coming victory should make our artists realise the pure noble quality of French blood. We have a whole intellectual province to reconquer. And so, whilst Fate is turning over the pages, Music must meditate in patience, before she breaks the affecting silence which will ensue after the bursting of the last shell . . .

Yet, thoughts of death soon returned. He wrote to Durand on 26 March: 'My poor mother died yesterday at half past one o'clock. Her struggle was long, although it seems she was without suffering. But does one know what happens at such moments?' He felt that he had little time left to accomplish what he saw as his mission to create a new French music. There is a hint of desperation in this letter to Valléry-Radot:

I have still so much to say. There are so many things in music which have never been done yet – for example, the human voice – I don't think it has been fully exploited up to now.

But all he could do was revise some of his old *Chansons de Bilitis* for piano duet, which were published that year under the title *Six Épigraphes antiques*, and appear in one concert as accompanist. Then, in June, worn out by the claustrophobia of wartime Paris, he and his family left for a holiday at Pourville near Dieppe.

The change of scene worked wonders. He had described his study in the Bois de Boulogne as a 'workshop of nothing', but now he was able to compose again. He wrote to Godet: 'I am writing like a madman, or one who knows he must die the next morning'; and: 'I want to work, not so much for myself, but to give proof, however small it may be, that even if there were thirty million Boches, French thought will not be destroyed.' Inspired by the Chopin he was editing, he produced a set of twelve studies of his own for piano. Writing to his publisher he said he was satisfied at having:

successfully realised a work which, if I may say so without false vanity, will always have a special place. For apart from purely technical considerations these studies will help pianists to understand that if they wish to enter the musical arena they will have to have a formidable pair of hands . . . not one is designed for the delight of pianists . . . They will frighten the fingers.

This was the first work in a new abstract vein. There are no picturesque titles to any of these *Études* as though he were re-evaluating the classical past and attempting to revive it in himself. He followed this work with a three-movement piece for two pianos, *En blanc et noir*. The black and white of the title is enigmatic, but seems appropriate to the bleakness Debussy felt had fallen, not only on Europe, but on the whole cultural climate of which he had formed so significant a part. If the *Épigraphes antiques* were a nostalgic farewell to the hedonistic Debussy, with their references to the death of the naiades in a harsh winter, the *Études* and *En blanc et noir* uncompromisingly faced a stark future of public destruction and private agony. The news of the death of Durand's cousin Lieutenant Jacques Charlot in the inconclusive spring offensive inspired the second movement, which is dedicated to him. In this very private music the sound of bugle calls are imitated on the keyboard with a reference to a chorale by Martin Luther which is dismissed by music that, as Debussy wrote to Durand, 'cleanses the atmosphere . . . of its poisonous fumes . . . or rather what it represents', and, in a preface to the score, Debussy quoted from François Villon's *Ballad Written Against the Enemies of France*.

Having exorcised some of his more deeply felt emotions, Debussy then began to consider how he might put his new ideas on the French classical tradition into practice. He turned to the concept of chamber music and planned six sonatas to be written for various combinations of instruments which would synthesise the art of Rameau, Couperin and their contemporaries with a twentieth-century idiom. He wrote the first two sonatas quickly. The Cello Sonata is an ironic piece in two movements. As well as alluding to earlier works, including *The Sunken Cathedral* in an obvious reference to the overwhelming of European culture, he drew his inspiration from the *Commedia dell'Arte* that had so inspired artists and musicians in the early years of the twentieth century with its bitter-sweet archetypes of human character, originally intending to call it 'Pierrot angry with the moon'. The other sonata finished that summer was a trio for the unusual but happy combination of flute, viola and harp. The tradition of flute and harp music is something peculiarly French. Ravel's famous *Introduction et Allegro* preceded the Debussy work by some ten years and later works by Guy Ropartz, Roussel and others continued the tradition, but the bewitching sounds that Debussy drew from his three contrasted instruments blended the hedonist in him with his 'latest experiments in musical chemistry', as he was fond of terming it. When he sent the scores to Durand he instructed him to print 'Claude Debussy – *musicien français*' on the title pages in an upsurge of pride in his nation and its culture.

He planned a Violin Sonata and another for the daring combination of oboe, horn and clavecin (harpsichord) and, feeling that he was progressing in a truly French idiom, he wrote to Stravinsky concerning German music as exemplified by Schoenberg's *Pierrot Lunaire*:

We must clear this insidious harvest from the face of the earth, we must destroy this bacteria of imitation grandeur and systematic ugliness. I know that you're one of the people who can fight and overcome all these types of gas which are just as lethal as the kind we know but which we've no gas masks to protect us from.

Yet, just when he was working so well, Debussy's illness began to give him such pain that he had to return to Paris for treatment. Writing to Durand in October from Pourville, he said:

I am enjoying these last days of liberty. I think of Paris as a sort of prison where one has not even the right to think and where even the walls have ears . . . Now the curtains have gone from the windows and when I see a trunk it makes me feel as sad as a cat.

His premonition was to be correct: these were the last real days of the composer's liberty. His return to Paris marked the beginning of the end.

A French village destroyed during the First World War

12 Last Days

The second autumn and winter of the war saw little change in the situation on the Western Front. The numbing trench slaughter continued without an inch being gained by either side. In this atmosphere of gloom, Debussy was told by a Parisian specialist that he would have to undergo a colostomy operation in December to help check the cancer which had spread throughout his lower intestine. He wrote to his friend Arthur Hartmann, the violinist with whom he had thought of touring America:

Of course this illness had to come at the end of a spell of good work . . . And in addition to all this misery, there were four months of those morphine injections that turn you into a walking corpse and completely annihilate your will . . . I was ready to work like a whole plantation of negroes and was preparing to write that violin and piano sonata you are kindly looking forward to . . . But now I do not know when the impulse to write will return. There are times when I feel as if I had never known anything about music . . .'

And later in the year:

Why was I not taught to polish spectacle glasses like Spinoza? I should never have had to depend on music for my daily bread.

The bitter winter of 1915 to 1916 brought reports of the destruction of whole villages in Belgium and Northern France. This so preyed on Debussy's already distressed mind that he poured out his feelings in one harrowing song, *Noël des enfants qui n'ont plus de maisons* (The Homeless Children's Christmas). He wrote both words and music and also arranged it for children's choir before undergoing the surgeon's knife.

The operation was only a partial success. He also had to undergo radium treatment. Now virtually an invalid, he was tended by his wife in the seclusion of their home. He wrote nothing at this time except letters. In June he wrote to Durand:

Life has become too hard and Claude Debussy, writing no more music, has no longer any reason to exist. I have no hobbies, they never taught me anything but music.

But later he wrote with determination:

I have made up my mind to ignore my health, to get back to work and to be no longer the slave of this over-tyrannical disease. We shall soon see. If I am doomed to disappear soon, I wish to have at least tried to do my duty.

In this anguished frame of mind he turned naturally to *The Fall of the House of Usher*. He recast the libretto, toning down the undramatic monologue element and giving more weight to Roderick's sister and the sinister doctor, bringing out the incest motif more strongly and introducing other effects from Poe including a raven that, as Debussy wrote in the libretto: 'passes through the fog and shakes its black wings like a funeral hand'. He may have continued working on the music in the summer of 1916, for a substantial amount of it, including almost the whole of the first scene in short score, has been discovered in private collections and reassembled in recent years after being thought almost totally lost. A reconstruction producing a performing edition of this fragment was made in 1976 by the composer Juan Allende-Blin and has since been broadcast on the radio. Although much, including the scoring, is conjectural, it is valuable in showing Debussy's mature touch. It is from the same stable as *Jeux* and *Le Martyre de saint-Sébastien* and its masterful use of atmosphere and vocal declamation produces exactly that obsessive 'progression of anguish' that haunts the story and haunted Debussy for more than ten years. If ever considered more than just a musical curiosity, it might be satisfactorily coupled with Bartók's *Duke Bluebeard's Castle* on stage – a work contemporaneous with it and sharing the same atmosphere of Symbolism and psychological obsession. The war was torturing artists of all kinds, but whilst the anguish of a Bluebeard or Roderick Usher was transformed by the Western Front into a scream of 'Anti-Art' by the Dada manifesto in 1916, this was also the year when that grand master of Impressionism, Monet, painted a cool, lucid series of *Waterlilies* in his garden near Paris as a testament to the sanity the world had temporarily lost.

Debussy was too ill to leave Paris that summer, but in October he felt sufficiently improved to travel with his family to Le Moulleau-Arcachon, near Cap Férat in the South of France. The Battle of the Somme and the year-long Battle of Verdun showed some improvement in the Allied position, but at a terrible price in lives, yet, amongst the light and landscapes he had known as a child, Debussy forgot the war sufficiently to begin sketching ideas

Claude Debussy and Chou Chou at Moulleau near Arcachon, 1916

116

for his *Violin Sonata*, although he soon suffered a relapse. He wrote to Durand:

Le Moulleau has not been able to help me and I shall not bring back any masterpieces. I might have a few sketches to be used later. I have never found hotel life so unpleasant. Even the walls are hostile – not to speak of this life in a numbered box.

He returned to Paris at the end of October and, in his home surroundings, took up the *Violin Sonata* again. He worked intermittently on it during the winter and early spring of 1917, only breaking off to involve himself in a patriotic project with his friend Laloy. *Ode à la France*, a reworking of the Joan of Arc story, was to be a choral work to words supplied by Laloy, and when Debussy received the first sections, he immediately sketched out the music in short score and continued working as and when he received other verses. He was not destined to finish it, however. An incomplete version was discovered after his death and eventually reconstructed and scored ten years later by Marius-François Gaillard. It was performed at the *Salle Pleyel* in Paris, but was regarded by many as an unworthy tribute to a composer who had written the sketch quickly during a period of great mental and physical distress.

Some of the strain may be discerned in the last work Debussy completed. The *Violin Sonata* was finished in March, though not without a great deal of effort and the rejection of at least one finale. Writing to Godet, Debussy said modestly that the work might be interesting 'from a documentary point of view and as an example of what a sick man can write in time of war'.

Following Debussy's successful editing of Chopin and knowing he was engaged in a violin sonata, Debussy's publisher asked him to edit J. S. Bach's violin sonatas. Debussy found the task uncongenial, writing to Durand:

. . . his marvellous style of writing . . . does not succeed in filling the awful void, which increases in proportion as he insists, at all costs, in turning some insignificant idea to account.

Debussy appeared as pianist at a concert in aid of French troops in March 1917, but did not perform the sonata until 5 May at the *Salle Gaveau* with, not Hartmann, but Gaston Poulet playing the violin part. André Suarès has left a pen portrait of the composer's last appearances on the Parisian concert stage:

I was very much struck not so much by his wasted, emaciated appearance, as by his absent-minded, weary expression. His face was like wax and the colour of ashes. The flame of fever did not glitter in his eyes, their light suggested the dull reflections from a pool. There was no bitterness in his gloomy smile, but rather the utter weariness of suffering . . . His hand, which was rounded, soft, plump, episcopal, weighed down his arm, his arm dragged down his whole body and on that head weighed life itself, unique, exquisite and cruel. A few people affected to speak of him with confidence, and found him in better health than they had expected . . . he looked at the audience with dull eyes from under flickering lids . . . He was overwhelmed with confusion, as alone an artist can be who loathes and is almost ashamed of suffering. It was even said that he allowed his disease to develop through concealing it. The voluptuous are often more anxious than others to hide their bodies, especially if they are blemished . . .

In the summer, Debussy underwent a second operation, but this could only check the progress of the illness for a few months; yet, despite his sufferings, he still considered new projects. Inspired by a performance of an obscure rewriting of *The Merchant of Venice* entitled *Shylock*, for which Fauré had provided some fine incidental music, Debussy discussed collaborating with the mercurial poet Toulet once more, writing incidental music for *As You Like It*, no doubt to be rewritten in much the same manner. Nothing came of this, however, nor of the opera on an East Indian theme that d'Annunzio proposed in a letter sent to Debussy from Fiume where he had become military governor. The Italian poet looked forward in the warmest terms to seeing Debussy again

Claude Debussy in St-Jean-de-Luz, 1917

when the war should be over, but it was not to be. Debussy also considered a series of miniature concertos in the same vein as his sonatas but, once more, these were only the plans of a fertile mind unable to discipline a sick body.

In June he was in the audience for a concert conducted by Molinari where he heard *La Mer* in an excellent performance. Then, in July, as a rest from Paris, the Debussys once more took a holiday in the South of France, at Saint Jean-de-Luz in the Pyrenees, hoping the mountain air would aid Debussy's convalescence. From there, Debussy wrote to Durand:

Up till now I've been horribly tired. My last illness has left me with an aversion to doing anything. There are mornings when dressing is like one of the twelve labours of Hercules. I long for anything to happen that would save me the trouble, even a revolution or an earthquake. Without being unduly pessimistic, I may say that my life is a hard one. I have to fight against illness and myself . . . I feel a nuisance to everyone . . .

Poulet visited him at the resort and Debussy managed to appear for one last concert, playing the *Violin Sonata* with him. The work was greatly applauded with an encore of the second movement demanded. Whilst in Saint Jean-de-Luz, Debussy also heard the legendary pianist Francis Planté, then in his seventies. He included excerpts from Debussy's *Pour le piano* and the first set of *Images* in two concerts, and Debussy was delighted at his understanding of the works.

Debussy returned to Paris in the autumn. There he arranged a selection of his articles for publication in book form under the title *Monsieur Croche, the Dilettante Hater*, but delays at the printers caused by wartime shortages prevented its publication until 1921. He also sent his revised libretto for *The Fall of the House of Usher* to his publisher and seemed once more ready to consider working on this opera, writing to Godet: 'This house has a curious resemblance to the House of Usher, although I haven't the mind troubles of Roderick . . . we are alike in our supersensitiveness', yet when the composer Alfred Bruneau visited him in October, he noticed some musical sketches on the piano which Debussy dismissed saying: 'I can no longer compose.' To Robert Godet he wrote at last: 'To tell the truth, I go on with this waiting life – waiting-room life, I might say, for I am a poor traveller waiting for a train that will never come again.'

The winter of 1917 to 1918, the last of the war, was particularly severe, all the more so as Paris was short of food and fuel due to a series of strikes and the loss of so much coal-mining and agricultural territory in the north. Debussy suffered badly. His illness now forced him to take to his room and finally to bed – 'In bed, always in bed!' he complained to visitors. The news of the slaughter of the French infantry in an abortive offensive was followed by the Allies being pushed beyond the Marne once again. As Debussy declined, the Germans came closer to Paris. Although their progress was halted, they were near enough to launch a series of air raids from zeppelins and unleash a new and terrifying weapon, the 'Big Bertha' long-range cannon on the capital. The first bombs exploded in the streets and outside Debussy's home on 23 March, but he was in too much pain to be carried to the safety of the basement. Two days later, at 10.00pm, he died in the middle of an air raid, with his wife and friends André Caplet and Valléry-Radot beside him.

At that time no one could foresee that Marshal Foch's offensive the following month would push the Germans back until, in November, they would surrender, worn out by the struggle. France would go wild with joy then, but Debussy had no inkling of victory – defeat was in the air when he died during what must have been the darkest days of the war for a *musicien français*.

Only a few colleagues on leave from the Front were able to attend his funeral which was held three days after he died. Louis Laloy was among them and left this moving account:

As in a bad dream, I can see the musicians in their soldiers' uniforms and the coffin near the piano. The door kept opening and closing and there was no room for flowers. The Minister of Education took his place at the head of the procession. Before me, side by side, Camille Chevillard and Gabriel Pierné, the conductors of our great philharmonic societies, walked in silence. All those concerts in which they had taken care of his music were over. The sky was overcast. In the distance was rumbling, was it a storm or an explosion? Along the wide avenues only military trucks could be seen. The people on the pavements pressed ahead quickly, but there was still a bustle in the populous uphill streets of Montmartre. The children made way and stood in line in the gutter and stared at us. The shopkeepers glanced at the streamers on the wreaths saying, 'It seems he was a musician.'

Of the fifty or so mourners who had set out, only a handful arrived at the Père Lachaise cemetery where many of the Paris Communards had been shot in 1871. There, a brief funeral oration concluded the gloomy rites. Shortly afterwards, Debussy's body was re-interred at the Passy cemetery.

★ ★ ★ ★

Many of Debussy's musical colleagues outlived him: Ravel, and old opponents including Saint-Saëns, Charpentier, Fauré and d'Indy, as well as friends including Dukas, Satie, Falla and Florent Schmitt. The younger generation of composers who were to further his experiments in post-war modernism included Roussel, and Stravinsky who was to survive into the second half of the new century. Debussy's widow lived another sixteen years, treasuring his memory and giving away odd manuscript pages from her husband's unfinished scores as keepsakes to his friends – a habit that has led to great confusion amongst those scholars attempting to discover which of Debussy's many abandoned works could be adequately completed. His beloved daughter Chou-Chou did not survive her father for long: she died during an epidemic of diphtheria in 1919.

At the time of his death, newsprint was scarce and confined to detailed accounts of the war. His passing was barely mentioned in French newspapers for several weeks: most tributes came from abroad. England, Italy and Spain produced the most effusive, whilst even obituaries in German newspapers honoured his memory as a great artist. It was not until May that two meagre reviews appeared in Paris journals. One appraised his art as essentially French, the other as ever-refined and limited in appeal.

This seemed to be typical. In the post-war years, although he had many champions, there were some who chose to denigrate him. Stung by his barbed wit and his ironic disdain, they wrote memoirs about his bohemian days when he had offended many. He had 'borrowed' the odd item (a green silk tie or the occasional overlooked sum of cash); a woman, claiming to be his mistress and as adept at dramatics as Debussy himself, had 'fainted' only to 'wake' and find him rifling her pockets. He cheated at cards. Whatever the truth of these tales, they can only throw a genius into human relief and perhaps a man who could occasionally be arrogant, snobbish, secretive and reserved invited a scandalous profile. But the enduring loyalty of those who were fascinated by his wit and charm remains. His friends worked tirelessly to keep his music before the public eye and, some years after his death, Debussy's first wife – the abandoned Gaby – was seen attending a lecture on the composer's life and works, long after colleagues who refused to forgive him for his treatment of her had faded into the shadows.

Opinions will always be divided over the greatest artists yet, despite the actions of the private man, his controversial life and obscure end, Debussy's reputation as a major composer, the 'father of modern music', is still assured.

Le Tombeau de Claude Debussy: a tribute to Debussy from fellow composers

Appendix

Debussy wrote criticism at irregular intervals from 1901 to 1914 and it is a fine indication of his wit and opinions, although often couched in the decadent prose of the authors he admired. His other literary efforts included part of a play, librettos to unfinished operas and the texts of several of his songs.

This appendix includes a short selection from his articles, some of which he later collected in *Monsieur Croche the Dilettante Hater*.

ON THE SYMPHONY

Recently the *Choral Symphony* was performed together with several of Richard Wagner's highly-spiced masterpieces. Once again Tannhäuser, Siegmund and Lohengrin voiced the claims of the *Leitmotiv*! The stern and loyal mastery of our great Beethoven easily triumphed over this vague and high-flown charlatanism.

It seems to me that the proof of the futility of the symphony has been established since Beethoven. Indeed, Schumann and Mendelssohn did no more than respectfully repeat the same forms with less power. The Ninth Symphony none the less was a demonstration of genius, a sublime desire to augment and to liberate the usual forms by giving them the harmonious proportions of a fresco.

Beethoven's real teaching then was not to preserve the old forms, still less to follow his early steps. We must throw wide the windows to the open sky; they seem to me to have only just escaped being closed for ever. The fact that here and there a genius succeeds in this form is but a poor excuse for the laborious and stilted compositions which we are accustomed to call symphonies.

The young Russian school has endeavoured to give new life to the symphony by borrowing ideas from popular melodies; it has succeeded in cutting brilliant gems; but are not the themes entirely disproportionate to the developments into which they have been forced? Yet the fashion for popular airs has spread quickly throughout the musical world – from east to west the tiniest villages have been ransacked and simple tunes, plucked from the mouths of hoary peasants, find themselves, to their consternation, trimmed with harmonic frills. This gives them an appearance of pathetic discomfort, but a lordly counterpoint ordains that they shall forget their peaceful origin.

Must we conclude that the symphony, in spite of so many attempted transformations, belongs to the past by virtue of its studied elegance, its formal elaboration and the philosophical and artificial attitude of its audience? Has it not in truth merely replaced its old tarnished frame of gold with the stubborn brass of modern instrumentation?

A symphony is usually built up on a chant heard by the composer as a child. The first section is the customary presentation of the theme on which the composer proposes to work; then begins the necessary dismemberment; the second section seems to take place in an experimental laboratory; the third section cheers up a little in a quite childish way interspersed with deeply sentimental phrases during which the chant withdraws as is more seemly; but it reappears and the dismemberment goes on; the professional gentlemen, obviously interested, mop their brows and the audience calls the composer. But the composer does not appear. He is engaged in listening to the voice of tradition which prevents him, it seems to me, from hearing the voice that speaks within him.

ON WAGNER

. . . Wagner's art can never completely die. It will suffer that inevitable decay, the cruel brand of time on all beautiful things; yet noble ruins must remain, in the shadow of which our grand-children will brood over the past splendour of this man who, had he been a little more human, would have been altogether great.

In *Parsifal*, the final effort of a genius which compels our homage, Wagner tried to drive his music on a looser rein and let it breathe more freely. We have no longer the distraught breathless-ness that characterises Tristan's morbid passion or Isolde's wild screams of frenzy; nor yet the grandiloquent commentary on the inhumanity of Wotan. Nowhere in Wagner's music is a more serene beauty attained than in the prelude to the third act of *Parsifal* and in the entire Good Friday episode; although, it must be admitted that Wagner's peculiar conception of human nature is also shown in the attitude of certain characters in this drama. Look at Amfortas, that melancholy Knight of the Grail who whines like a shop girl and whimpers like a baby. Good heavens! A Knight of the Grail, a king's son, would plunge his spear into his own body rather than parade a guilty wound in doleful melodies for three acts! As for Kundry, that ancient rose of hell, she has furnished much copy for Wagnerian literature; and I confess I have but little affection for such a sentimental draggle-tail. Klingsor is the finest character in *Parsifal*: a quondam Knight of the Grail, sent packing from the Holy Place because of his too pronounced views on chastity. His bitter hatred is amazing; he knows the worth of men and scornfully weighs the strength of their vows of chastity in the balance. From this it is obvious that this crafty magician, this old gaol-bird, is not merely the only human character in this drama, in which the falsest moral and religious ideas are set forth, ideas of which the youthful Parsifal is the heroic and insipid champion.

Here in short is a Christian drama in which nobody is willing to sacrifice himself, though sacrifice is one of the highest of the Christian virtues! If Parsifal recovers his miraculous spear, it is thanks to old Kundry, the only creature actually sacrificed in the story: a victim twice over, once to the diabolical intrigues of Klingsor and again to the sacred spleen of a Knight of the Grail. The atmosphere is certainly religious, but why have the incidental children's voices such sinister harmonies? Think for a moment of the childlike candour that would have been conveyed if the spirit of Palestrina had been able to dictate its expression.

The above remarks only apply to the poet whom we are accustomed to admire in Wagner and have nothing to do with the musical beauty of the opera, which is supreme. It is incomparable and bewildering, splendid and strong. *Parsifal* is one of the loveliest monuments of sound ever raised to the serene glory of music.

[Wagner was] a beautiful sunset that was mistaken for a dawn . . .

ON MUSSORGSKY

It is evident that he had not very long for the development of his genius; and he lost no time, for he will leave an indelible impression on the minds of those who love him or will love him in the future. No one has given utterance to the best within us in tones more gentle or more profound: he is unique, and will remain so, because his art is spontaneous and free from arid formulas. Never has a more refined sensibility been conveyed by such simple means; it is like the art of an enquiring savage discovering music step by step through his emotions. Nor is there ever a question of any particular form; at all events the form is so varied that by no possibility whatsoever can it be related to any established, one might say official, form, since it depends on and is made up of successive minute touches mysteriously linked together by means of an instinctive clairvoyance . . .

ON REMOVING THE MYSTIQUE OF MUSIC

At a time like ours, in which mechanical skill has attained unsuspected perfection, the most famous works may be heard as easily as one may drink a glass of beer, and it only costs ten centimes, like the automatic weighing machines. Should we not fear this domestication of sound, this magic that anyone can bring from a disc at his will? Will it not bring to waste the mysterious force of an art which one might have thought indestructible? Why don't they understand that there is really no reason to have so many centuries of music behind us, to have thus profited by this magnificent intellectual heritage and to seek childishly to rewrite history? Is not our duty, on the contrary, to find the symphonic music appropriate to our age, that which is demanded by progress, bravery and modern victories? The century of aeroplanes has a right to a music of its own.

★ ★ ★ ★

Debussy contributed to: *La Revue Blanche* (April-December 1901); *Gil Blas* (January-June 1903); *Musica* (October 1902, May 1903); *Le Mercure de France* (January 1903); *La Revue Blanche* (March-April 1904, June 1906); *Le Figaro* (May 1908); *Comoedia* (June 1908, November 1909, January 1910); *Le Paris Journal* (May 1910); *Revue S.I.M.* (November 1912-March 1914).

Selected Bibliography

Vallas, L: *Claude Debussy, His Life and Works* (Oxford 1933)

Peter, R: *Claude Debussy* (Paris 1931)

Laloy, L: *Debussy* (Paris 1909)

Koechlin, C: *Debussy* (Paris 1941)

Oleggini, L: *Le Cas de Claude Debussy* (Paris 1947)

Lockspeiser, E: *Debussy* (Master Musicians Series, London 1963)

Lockspeiser, E: *Debussy et Edgar Poe* (Paris, 1962)

Debussy, C: *Monsieur Croche the Dilettante Hater* (New York 1928)

Nijinsky, R. (Ed): *The Diary of Vaslav Nijinsky* (London 1963)

Tosi, G. (Ed): *Debussy et d'Annunzio : Correspondance inédite* (Paris 1948)

Lettres de Claude Debussy à son editeur (Paris 1927)

Correspondance de Claude Debussy et Pierre Louÿs 1893-1904 (Paris 1945)

Correspondance de Claude Debussy et P-J. Toulet (Paris 1929)

Lettres de Claude Debussy à Deux Amis (Paris 1942)

Selective Listing of Works

ORCHESTRAL
Printemps
Prélude à l'après-midi d'un faune
Nocturnes: Nuages, Fêtes, Sirènes
La Mer
Images:
   Gigues (orch. Caplet)
   Ibéria
   Rondes de printemps
Incidental music for King Lear: Fanfare, Sommeil de Lear
Fantaisie for piano and orchestra
Danse sacrée et danse profane for harp and strings
Jeux: ballet
Khamma: ballet (orch. Koechlin)
La Boîte à joujoux: ballet (orch. Caplet)
Rapsodie for saxophone and orchestra (orch. Roger-Ducasse)
Première Rapsodie for clarinet and orchestra (orch. Debussy)
Danse (Tarentelle styrienne) (orch. Ravel)
Berceuse héroïque
La Plus que lente
Marche écossaise
Children's Corner Suite (orch. Caplet)
Petite Suite (orch. Büsser)

OPERA
Pelléas et Mélisande

CHORAL WORKS
Le Gladiateur – cantata (unpublished)
L'Enfant prodigue – cantata
   Cortège et Danse
La Damoiselle élue – cantata

Le Martyre de Saint-Sébastien (orch. Caplet)
Ode à la France (completed Gaillard)
Salut, printemps (unpublished)
Trois Chansons de Charles d'Orléans for unaccompanied chorus
Diane au Bois (unpublished)

Intermezzo (unpublished)

Zuleima (unpublished)

CHAMBER
Nocturne for violin and piano (unpublished)
Scherzo for violin and piano (unpublished)
String Quartet in G minor
Sonata for cello and piano
Sonata for flute, viola and harp
Sonata for violin and piano
Trio for piano, violin and cello (unpublished)
Chansons de Bilitis for 2 flutes, 2 harps and celesta (unpublished)

PIANO
Danse bohémienne
Deux Arabesques
Rêverie
Ballade
Danse
Images oubliées
Suite bergamasque
Pour le piano
Estampes
D'un cahier d'esquisses
Images (first series)
Images (second series)
Masques
L'Île joyeuse
Children's Corner Suite
Preludes (first set)
    The Girl with the Flaxen Hair
    The Sunken Cathedral
Preludes (second set)
Études (book one)
Études (book two)
Petite Suite (piano duet)
Marche écossaise (The Earl of Ross March) (piano duet)
Six Épigraphes antiques (piano duet)
En blanc et noir (two pianos)

SONGS
Cinq Poèmes de Baudelaire
Ariettes oubliées
Le jet d'eau
Fêtes galantes (two sets)
Trois Chansons de Bilitis
Trois Chansons de France
Le Promenoir des deux amants
Trois Ballades de François Villon
Trois Poèmes de Stéphane Mallarmé
Noël des enfants qui n'ont plus de maisons (words by Debussy)

UNFINISHED WORKS
Rodrigue et Chimène – opera
The Fall of the House of Usher – opera
The Devil in the Belfry – opera

Index

*Illustrations are indicated by **bold** type*

Académie 25, 28, 37, 39
Académie des Beaux Arts 107
Adam, Villiers de Lisle 29
Adonis 95, 97
Aesthetes 54
Aesthetic Movement 32, 54, 84
Africa 32, 38
A la Recherche du Temps Perdu 59, 103
Albéniz, Isaac 55, 72, 89, 90, 106
  Ibéria 89
Alhambra, The 72, 106
Alkan, Charles 10
Allen, Maud 100, 101
Allende-Blin, Juan 116
Alphaud, Avenue 75
America 84, 85, 115
Amfortas 126
Amsterdam 107
Anély, Max 91
Annam 38
Annamite Orchestras 38
Annamite Pavilion 37
Annamite Theatre 38
Annunzio, Gabriele d' 95, 97, 99, 119
Anti-Art 103, 116
Antoine 74
Après-midi d'un faune, L' (text) 42, **47**
Arkel 49
Arosa, Achille-Antoine 6, **7**, 13
Art Nouveau 52
Asia, South-East 32
As You Like It 68, 119
Auber, Daniel 51
Auberge du Clou 41
Austro-Hungarian Empire 93, 94, 107
Avray, Ville d' 17, 18

Bach, J. C. 118
  Violin Sonatas 118
Bailly, Edmond 34, 43
Bakst, Leon 89, 91, 97, 99, 191, 103, 105
Balakirev, Mily 19
Balinese Orchestras 38
Ballad Written Against the Enemies of France 113
Ballets Russes, The 89, 91, 92, 100, 102
Banville, Theodore de 9, 11, 21, 25, 27
Barbizon Group 6
Bardac, Emma (Mme Debussy) 72, 73, 74, 75, 76, **76**, 121, 122
Bardac, Raoul 72
Bardac, Sigismond 74
Baron, Emile 27
Barrès, Antoine 11
Bartók, Bela 116

Duke Bluebeard's Castle 116
Battersea 53
Baudelaire, Charles 53, 25, 43, 88, 93
Bauer, Harold 85
Bayreuth 20, 31, 36, **36**, 67
Bedier, M. 91
Beethoven, Ludwig van 11, 13, 40, 42, 44, 125
  Pastoral Symphony 69
  Choral Symphony 125
Belgium 109, 115
Bellaigue, Camille 11
Belsize Park 54
Berlin 84, 103
Berlioz, Hector 13
Bichain 67, 70
'Big Bertha' 121
Biron, Hôtel 102
Bismarck 8
Bizet, Georges 17
  Carmen 17, 32
Blake, William 48
Blessed Damozel, The 43
Bluebeard 82, 116
Bois de Boulogne 72, 76, **76**, 83, 87, 92, 96, 112
Boito, Arrigo 25
  Mefistofele 25
Bonheur, Raymond 21, 50
Bordeaux 110
Borodin, Alexander 19, 20
  Prince Igor 38, 89
  Polovtsian Dances 89
Boston 68, 99
Botticelli 26, 27
Boudin 6
Boulanger, General 46
Boulevard des Italiens 42
Bourgeat, General 64
Brahms, Johannes 32, 34, 94
Brasserie Pousset 57, **57**, 58, 59
Britain 109
Bruneau, Alfred 46, 60, 89, 120
  Messidor 46
Brussels 44, 45, 82
Budapest 94
Burgundy 57, 70
Büsser, Henri 93, 103
Byblus 95

Cabat 24, 26
Cabourg 93
Cakewalk, The 75, 85
Calvocoressi, M.D. 78
Campanini 88
Cannes 6
Cap Férat 116
Caplet, André 95, 100, 103, 106, 121
Cardinet, Rue 58
Carnot, President 46

Carré, Albert 56, 62
Caruso, Enrico 92
Cas Debussy, Le 88
Câteau, Le 110
Ceinture 83
Cendruline 45, 56
Central Colonial Palace **37**
Cézanne 41, 75
Chabrier, Alexis 26, 67, 89, 90, 100
  España 89
  Gwendoline 31, 67
  Valses romantiques 26
Champs de Mars 37, 60
Charleroi 110
Charlot, Jacques 112
Charpentier, Gustave 59, 121
  Louise 59, 60, 63, 72
Château de Chenonceaux, Interlaken 14
Châtelet, The 89, 91, 92, 95, 97, 99, 105
Chat Noir, Le 7, 34, **35**, 59
Chaussée d'Antin 34
Chausson, Ernest 31, 42, 43, 44, 45, 49, **50**, 52, 58, 67, 77
  Le Roi Arthus 31, 67
Chausson, Mme. **50**
Chevillard, Camille 76, 121
Chez Weber 59
Chopin, Frédéric 5, 7, 8, 10, 11, 13, 79, 92, 111, 112, 118
  Ballade No. 2 11
  Piano Concerto No. 2 11
  Polonaises 110
  Waltzes 110
Christ 95, 99
Cimbalom, The 94
City in the Sea, The 92
Classicism 26, 35
Claudel, Paul 29
Clichy 5
Colette 91
Colonne, Concerts 31, 74, 80, 89, 103
Columbine 27
Commedia dell' Arte 26, 39, 113
Commune, The 8, 110, 121
Comoedia 99, 128
Concordia, La 17
Conservatoire, Paris 7, 8, 9, **9**, 11, 13, 14, 15, 16, 20, 21, 23, 29
Constantinople, Rue de 17
Corneau, André 66
Couperin, François 111, 113
Courrier Musicale 90
Courrier Undine 61
Covent Garden 69, 70, 84, 87
Croche, Monsieur, The Dilettante Hater 60, 61, 120, 125
Croix d'Honneur 67
Cui, César 19

Dada 116
Danilchenko **14**
Daphnis et Chloë 55
Debussy:
  Adèle 5-6
  Alfred 6
  Claude
    Birthplace: 6
    Portraits of the composer: **4, 7,**
    12, 14, 25, 28, 50, 58, 76, 91,
    105, 108, 117, 119
Debussy, Claude-Emma (Chou-Chou)
  76, **80,** 81, 83, 85, 105, 106, 116,
  117, 122
Debussy, Emmanuel 6
Debussy, Eugène 6
Debussy, Manuel-Achille 5, **5,** 6, 7, 8,
  11
Debussy, Victorine 5, **5,** 21, 67, 111
Debussyists 66, 67, 79
Décadence 55, 95
Delibes, Léo 12
Derain, André 75
Devil in the Belfry, The 67, 81, 84, 86,
  89, 92
Diaghilev, Serge 89, **89,** 91, 97, 102-3
Dieppe 112
Diocletian, Emperor 95
Don Juan 68
Doret, Gustave 46
Dreyfus, Captain 46
Duchamp, Marcel 103
Dukas, Paul 31, 37, 42, **42,** 47, 49, 55,
  66, 82, 100, 103, 105, 121
  Ariane et Barbe-bleu 82
  La Péri 105
  The Sorcerer's Apprentice 82
Duparc, Henri 49, 72
  Mélodies 72
Dupin, Étiénne 36, 39
Dupont, Gabrielle (Gaby) **33,** 34, 41,
  45, 50, 57, 58, 73, 122
Durand, Concerts 90
Durand, Emile 11, **11,** 13, 70
Durand, Jacques 75, 79, 80, 86, 88,
  90, 93, 97, 105, 109, 110, 111, 112,
  113, 115, 118, 120
Durbar, Delhi 100, 106

Eastbourne 75-6
Echo de Paris 43
Education, Minister of 121
Edward VII, King 87, 100
Eiffel Tower, The 37
Elgar, Edward 34, 100
  Symphony No. 2 100
Embarkation for Cythera, The 73
Emmanuel, Maurice 11
Empire, The Second 5, 8
England 54, 55, 75, 81, 84, 85, 87, 88,

89, 106, 107, 122
Entente Cordiale, The 87
Etruscan Tomb, The 23
Excelsior, The 96
Exposition Universelle 37, **37, 38,** 39,
  60, 68
Expressionists, The 75, 94

Falla, Manuel de 90, 121
  Nights in the Gardens of Spain 90
Fantin-Latour 32
Fauré, Gabriel 31, 42, 72, 73, 103,
  119, 121
  Ballade for Piano and Orchestra 69
  La Bonne Chanson 73
  Mélodies 72
  Pénélope 103
  Shylock 119
Fauves, The 75
Fêtes galantes 18
Figaro, Le 22, 47, 64, 128
Fine Arts, Ministry of 60
Fiume 119
Fiumicino 25
Five, The 19
Fleurville, Mme Mauté de 7, 8, **8,** 9, 111
Florence 15, **15,** 16
Foch, Marshal 121
Fokin, Mikhail 89
Fontainas, André 40
Forster, E. M. 48
France 7, 31, 32, 46, 52, 55, 81, 87,
  91, 97, 100, 104, 115, 121
France, South of 6, 15, 116, 120
Franck, César 13, **16,** 28, 31, 42, 45,
  52, 77, 81
Franco-Prussian War 8, 13, 109
Frères en Art, Les 73
Freud, Sigmund 94
Fromont 40
Fuller, Loie 103

Gaillard, Marius-François 118
Gallé, Emile 52
Gambara, Veronica 95
Garden, Mary 63, 65, **65,** 67, **67,** 83, 84
Gatti-Casazza, Giulio 84, 92
Gauguin, Paul 34
Gauthier-Villars, Henri ('Willy') 43,
  47, 91
George V, King 100
German, Edward 76
Germany 84, 107
Gide, André 29
Gil Blas 68, 128
Gilbert, W. S. 32
Godet, Robert 37, 67, 102, 110, 112,
  118, 120
Golaud 83
Gounod, Charles 5, 17, 22, 27, 31, 56, 66

Faust 5, 17
Grail, Knight of the 126
Grandes Baigneuses, Les 75
Grieg, Edvard 6
Guide Musicale 74
Guiraud, Ernest **16,** 17, 19, 20, 21, 29,
  36
Gustave Doré, Rue 34

Hague, The 107
Hahn, Reynaldo 59
Halévy, Jacques 5
Hall, Mrs Eliza 68, 74, 88
Hamlet 86, 97
Hammerstein, Oscar 84
Handel, George 34
Harlequin 27, 93
Hartmann, Arthur 85, 115, 118
Hartmann, Georges 40, 52, 64, 66
Haydn, Franz 45
Hébert 26, 27
Heine 20, 25, 27
Hellé, André 105, 107
Heroïque, Marche 110
Hokusai 69, 70
Holland 107
Hommage à E. A. Poe 32
Hôtel d'Alsace 59
Howards End 48
Hugo, Valentine 105
Huysmans, J. K. 30, 52

Impressionism 6, 12, 28, 29, 33, 34,
  61, 74, 81, 82, 89, 90, 106, 116
India 100
Indy, Vincent d' 31, 35, 39, 42, 55, 66
  68, 81, 82, 84, 103, 121
  Choral Varié 68
  Fervaal 67
Isolde 126
Italy 23, 84, 99, 122

J'accuse 46
Jersey 85
Joan of Arc 118
Jockey Club, The 61
Joffre, Marshal 110
Journal of International Music 106

Keel Row, The 89
King Albert's Album 110
Klimt, Gustav 94
Klingsor 127
Koechlin, Charles 101
Kokoschka, Oscar 94
Koussevitsky, Serge 106
Kufferath, Maurice 45
Kundry 127

Laforge, Jules 29

Lalo, Eduard 13, 66
  Namouna 13
  Roi d'Ys, Le 66, 93
Lalo, Pierre 66, 76
Laloy, Louis 75, 81, 105, 118, 121
Lamoureux Concerts 31, 60, 61, 69, 76
Lassus 27
Lavignac, Albert 10, 11
Leblanc, Georgette 63
Leclerq, Maurice 86, 88
Leitmotiv 41, 125
Leoncavallo, Ruggiero 25
  I Pagliacci 25
Lerolle, Henri 50, 51
Librairie de l'Art Indépendant 34
Liszt, Franz 5, **25**, 26
L'hermite, Tristan 91
Lohengrin 125
London 6, 32, 33, 42, **53**, 54, 55, 57, 69, 70, 75, 84, 85, 86, 87, 107
Londres, Rue de 34, 50, 58
Lorrain, Jean 66
Louvain 109
Louÿs, Pierre 32, 34, **34**, 40, 44, 45, 46, 51, 55, 56, 57, 58, 59, 67, 73
Luther, Martin 112

Maeterlinck, Maurice 42, 44, 50, 51, 63, **63**, 64, 82, 106
Magnard, Albéric 67
Mahler, Gustav 94
Malherbe, Henri 96
Mallarmé, Stéphane 18, 29, 31, **31**, 32, 42, 47, 48, 59, 106
Manet, Eduard 27, 29, 31, 47
Manhattan Opera House 84
Maöle, Martin van 88
Marmontel, Antoine 10, **10**, 11, 13, 14
Marne, River **50**, 110, 121
Mascagni, Pietro 59
Massenet, Jules 13, 15, 17, 21, 52, 56, 66
  Le Cid 40
  Hérodiade 13
  Manon 13
Mata Hari 59
Matin, Le 66, 89
Matisse, Henri 75
Mauclair, Camille 50, 51
Maupassant, Guy de 37
McMahon, Marshal 34
Mecks, von **18**, 19, 20, 23
Meck, Julia von 14
Meck, Nadezhda von 13, 14, 15, 16, 19
Meck, Nicholas von 15
Meck, Sophie von 106
Meck, Vladimir von 20
Mélisande 49, 52, 62, 64, **65**, 82, **83**
Mendelssohn, Felix 34, 125
Mendès, Catulle 40, **40**, 42, 57
Ménestral, Le 47

Merchant of Venice, The 118
Mercure de France, La 128
Messager, André 56, **56**, 57, 62, 64, 66, 67, 69, 73
Metro, The 52
Metropolitan Opera House 84, 86, 92
Meyerbeer, Giacomo 5
Molinari, Bernardino 120
Monet, Claude 41, 116
Mons 110
Monte Rotondo 23
Montesquiou Robert de 51, 52, **52**
Montmartre 7, 17, **30**, 34, 41, 45, 49, 59, 121
Moore, George 55
Moreau, Gustave 75
Moscow 19, **19**, 20, 106
Moulleau-Arcachon 116, **117**, 118
Moureau-Sainti, Mme 17
Mourey, Gabriel 81, 91
Mozart, W. A. 10, 13, 26, 44, 66
Munich 84
Musica 128
Musicians' Club, The 87
Musicien français 113, 121
Mussorgsky, Modest 19, 38, **39**, 66, 72, 127
  Boris Godunov 39
  Night on the Bare Mountain 38

Napoleon III, Emperor 5, 8
National School of Music 88
'New Music' 26
New York 92
New York Times 84
Nijinsky, Vaslav 89, 91, **101**, 102, 103
Novello's 32, 34
Nude Descending a Staircase 103

Odéon Theatre 74
Offenbach, Jacques 5, 12, 27, 34
  Tales of Hoffmann 17
Opéra, Paris 5, 91
Opéra-Comique 5, 12, 56, 61, 63, **65**, **66**, 81, 82, 83, 103
Orléans, Charles de 74
Orpheus (Orphée) 68, 91

Pachulsky **14**
Pain, Rue au 5, **6**
Palace of Electricity 60
Palestrina, Giovanni 27, 127
Panama Canal Company 46
Pan, Peter 106
Paris 5, 6, 8, 15, 16, 19, 20, 23, 24, 27, 28, 29, 30, 31, 32, 34, 36, 37, 40, 42, 44, 46, 49, 52, 54, 55, 56, 59, 67, 70, 73, 74, 75, 76, 83, 84, 85, 87, 89, 90, 92, 94, 99, 100, 103, 109, 110, 112, 113, 114, 116, 118, 120, 121, 122

Paris, Archbishop of 97, 99
Paris Journal, Le 56, 128
Parnasse Contemporain 9
Parry, Charles 34, 55
Parsifal 127
Pasdeloup Concerts 31
Passy 121
Pavillon des Muses 51, 52
Peking 91
Pélléas 52, **66**, 83
Pélléas et Mélisande (drama) 42, 43, 44, 49
Pélléastres 66
Pentatonic Scale 38
Père Lachaise Cemetery 121
Perrier, Jean **66**, 83
Pessard 12
Peter, René 34, 73
Petit Journal, Le 57
Pierné, Gabriel 10, 23, 121
Pierrot 113
Pigalle, Rue 5
Pissarro, Camille 13, 30
Planté, Francis 120
Podolsk 19
Poe, Edgar Allan 32, 32, 67, 81, 86, 88, 89, 90, 92, 95, 116
Pont des Arts, Le 22
Pope, The 23, 88
Poulet, Gaston 118, 120
Pour la Musique Française 111
Pourville 112, 113
Pre-Raphaelites, The 25, 27, 31, 32, 43, 57
Primoli, Count Josef 25
Prix de Rome 19, 20, 21, 22, 23, 55, 60
Promenade Concerts 84
Proust, Marcel 52, 59, **59**, 82, 103
Prussia 8
Puccini, Giacomo 59, 94
  La Bohème 59
Pulchinello 27, 88

Queen's Hall 84, 86

Radics 94
Raff, Joseph 40
Rameau, Jean 79, 111, 113
Ravel, Maurice 45, **54**, 55, 72, 81, 82, 90, 102, 109, 121
  Daphnis et Chloë 102
  Habañera (Sites Auriculaires) 55, 72
  Histoires Naturelles 82
  Introduction et Allegro 113
  Rapsodie Espagnole 72, 89
Realism 59
Rebours, A 30, 52
Redon, Odilon 29, 32, 75, 102
Regnier, Henri 34
Renaissance, The 95

Republic, Third 12, 46
Revue Blanche, La 60, 128
Revue Indépendante, La 27, 34
Revue S.I.M., La 106, 128
Revue wagnérienne, La **32**
Reynolds Bar 59
Richter, Hans 69
Rimbaud, Arthur 8, 9, 30, 32
Rimsky-Korsakov, Nicolai 19, 20, 38, 89
   Caprice Espagnole 39, 89
   Scheherazade 91, 97
Rodin, Auguste 102
Rodrigue et Chimène 40, 42
Roger, Thérèse 15
Roger-Ducasse, Jean 74, 90, 100
Rolland, Romain 32, 66
Rome 15, 16, 22, 23, 25, 27, 85, 106
Rome, Rue de 29
Ropartz, Guy 113
Rosicrucianism 41
Rossetti, Dante Gabriel 25, 27, 43, 55, 57
Rostan, Mme. (Octavie de la
   Ferronnière) 6
Rousseau, Theodore 6
Roussel, Albert 90, 113, 122
Rubinstein, Anton 20
Rubinstein, Ida 91, 95, 97, **98**, 99
Ruskin, John 29
Russia 19, 21, 38, 45, 106, 107

Sacré Coeur 34
St. Cecilia, Academy of 106
St. Germain-en-Laye 5, 6
St. Jean-de-Luz **119**, 120
St. Petersburg 106
Saint-Saëns, Camille 13, 26, 31, 52,
   54, 121
   Samson et Delilah 54
   Variations on a Theme of Beethoven
   26
St. Sebastian 95, 97, 98
Salle Gaveau 118
Salle Pleyel 118
San Maria dell'Anima 27
Sant' Agathe 25
Sarajevo, Serbia 109
Satie, Erik 41, 41, 56, 58, 109, 121
   Bureaucratic Sonata 41
   Gymnopédies 56
   Three Pear-shaped Pieces 41
Saulaie, La 55
Scala, La, Milan 84, 92
Schmitt, Florent 90, 100, 121
   La Tragedie de Salomé 100
Schoenberg, Arnold 36, 42, 94, 103
   Pierrot Lunaire 103, 113
Schola Cantorum 55, 81, 84
Schumann, Robert 11, 13, 79, 125
Ségalen, Victor 91
Sgambati 26

Shakespeare, William 25, 68
Shaw, Bernard 32
Sibelius, Jean 43
Siegmund 125
Sivry, Charles de 7
Société Musicale Indépendante, La 99
Société Nationale, La 39, 42, 44, 46,
   72, 80
Somme, Battle of the 116
Spain 72, 81, 89, 122
Speyer, Sir Edgar and Lady 107
Spinoza 115
Spiritualism 41
Stanford, Charles 34
Strauss, Richard 88, 100
Stravinsky, Igor 90, 100, 102, **105**,
   113, 122
   The Firebird 91
   Petrouchka 100, 105
   The Rite of Spring 105
Suarès, André 32, 118
Sullivan, Arthur 6, 32, 34, 55, 76
   HMS Pinafore 6
Swinburne, Algernon 81
Switzerland 14
Symbolism 18, 27, 29, 30, 31, 34, 42,
   59, 75, 95, 102, 116
Symphony, The 125-6
Symphony, The French 13, 77

Tchaikovsky, Peter 13, 14, 15, 19, 20
   Swan Lake 15
Telegraph, The Daily 110
Temps, Le 11
Texier, Rosalie (Mme. Debussy) 57,
   58, **58**, 60, 70, 72, 73, 74, 75, 76, 82
Teyte, Maggie 82, 83, **83**, 85, 100
Theater an der Wien **93**
Théâtre des Bouffes-Parisiens 43
Théâtre des Champs-Elysées 103, 105
Théâtre Marigny 106
Théâtrephone, The 82
Theosophy 41
Tombeau de Claude Debussy, Le 122,
   123
Tonkin 68
Toscanini, Arturo 92
Toulet, Paul-Jean 57, 68, 119
Toulouse-Lautrec, Henri de 41
Tristan 126
Tristan et Yseult 81, 84, 90, 91
Turner, J.M.W. 34, 89
Twelve-Tone Scale 36, 103
Tzigane, The 94

Ukraine, The 19
Usher, Roderick, 86, 88, 89, 96, 116,
   120
Usher, The Fall of the House of 32, 84,
   86, 88, 88, 89, 92, 97, 116, 120

Valéry, Paul 29
Valéry-Radot, Pasteur 105, 111, 112,
   121
Vasnier, Mme. 17, **17**, 18, 20, 22, 25
Vasnier, M. 18, 27, 28
Vasniers, The 23, 25, 27, 29
Vatican, The 23
Venice 20
Verdi, Giuseppe 25, 92
   Aida 92
   Falstaff 92
Verdun 110, 116
Verismo 59
Verlaine, Paul 8, 9, 18, 25, 29, 32, 36
   54
Versailles 8
Vidal, Paul 12, 17, 21, 23, 26
Vienna 20, 32, 93, **93**, 94
Villa Medici, The 15, 19, 22, 23, **24**,
   26, 28, 39, 106
Villon, François 91, 113
Viñes, Ricardo 72, 75, 80, 93
Vinteuil 59
Vuillermoz, Emile 80

Wagner, Richard 5, 7, 10, 20, **20**, 26,
   28, 31, 32, 36, 40, 42, 43, 48, 52,
   66, 67, 88, 125, 126-7
   Good Friday Music 126
   Die Meistersinger 36
   Parsifal 36, 99, 126-7
   The Ring 69, 70
   Tannhäuser 5, 10, 125
   Tristan und Isolde 20, 26, 36, 81
War Minister, French 99
Waterlilies 116
Watteau 73
Wave, The **69**, 70
Weingartner, Felix 68
Weismann, Jacques 91
Whistler, James McNeil 29, 30, 50,
   52, 53
Whole-Tone Scale 38, 68, 79
Wilde, Oscar 32, 54, 58, 72, 97
Wilhelm I, Kaiser 8
Wilhelm II, Kaiser 87, 109
Willowwood 55
Wood, Sir Henry 84
World War One 109-122 (passim)
   114
Wotan 126

Yeats, W.B. 103
Yellow Book, The 54
Ys, d' 92
Ysaÿe, Eugène 44, 50, 55, 56, 57
Ysaÿe Quartet, The 44, **44**, 45

Zion, The Priests of 41
Zola, Emile 32, 46, 59

Printed in Great Britain by Redwood Books   11/99(35806)